Learn for your life

A blueprint for career-long learning

Eddy Knasel, John Meed and Anna Rossetti

FINANCIAL TIMES
Prentice Hall

An imprint of **Pearson Education**
London · New York · San Francisco · Toronto · Sydney · Tokyo · Singapore · Hong Kong
Cape Town · Madrid · Paris · Milan · Munich · Amsterdam

Pearson Education Limited

Head Office:
Edinburgh Gate
Harlow CM20 2JE
Tel: +44 (0)1279 623623
Fax: +44 (0)1279 431059

London Office:
128 Long Acre, London WC2E 9AN
Tel: +44 (0)20 7447 2000
Fax: +44 (0)20 7240 5771
www.business-minds.com

First published in Great Britain 2000

© Eddy Knasel, John Meed and Anna Rossetti 2000

The right of Eddy Knasel, John Meed and Anna Rossetti to be identified as
Authors of this Work has been asserted by them in accordance with the
Copyright, Designs and Patents Act 1988.

ISBN: 0 273 64917 5

British Library Cataloguing in Publication Data
A CIP catalogue record for this book can be obtained from the British Library.

10 9 8 7 6 5 4 3 2 1

Designed by Claire Brodmann Book Designs, Burton-on-Trent
Typeset by M Rules
Printed and bound in Great Britain by Biddles Ltd, Guildford & King's Lynn

The Publishers' policy is to use paper manufactured from sustainable forests.

Contents

4 Becoming a powerful learner 65

5 The capable learner 85

6 The reflective learner 103

7 The creative learner 125

Author biographies

Anna Rossetti, John Meed and Eddy Knasel are the three partners in Learners First, a consultancy which is at the leading edge of national developments in work-related learning and which has worked for a wide range of companies, government departments and agencies and universities.

Anna Rossetti. Anna started work as a teacher of children with learning difficulties and soon became involved with the start of the adult literacy movement with the Workers Educational Association. She moved on to work as training manager and open learning writer and commissioning editor at the National Extension College in Cambridge. She believes passionately that most people do not achieve their full learning potential, that much formal education does not help them to do so and often serves to narrow their horizons.

Anna lives in Bristol where she divides her time between looking after her two daughters, helping with the local Woodcraft Folk group and working as a writer and researcher while dreaming about snorkelling and scuba diving over coral reefs.

John Meed. John began work with the Audio Visual Media Research Unit of the Open University, before moving on to join the National Extension College in Cambridge where he became Assistant Director for Education. John has been extensively involved in researching key educational issues and writing learning materials. He is the author of a number of management and education books including *The Intelligent Manager*, *Becoming Competent*, *Implementing Flexible Learning*, and *How to Study Effectively*.

John has two children, and his interests include pop music, playing flamenco guitar, walking, reading, cinema and eating.

Eddy Knasel. An occupational psychologist, Eddy studied at Bangor and Aston universities before moving to Cambridge to join the National Institute for Careers Education and Counselling, where he first became involved in work-based learning. He published his first book *Your Work in Your Hands* in 1986, shortly after leaving the Institute and becoming one-third of Learners First. More recently, he collaborated with Steve Morris and Graham Willcocks in writing *How to Lead a Winning Team* (FT Prentice Hall).

Eddy now lives in Bristol, within 30 seconds walk of the county cricket ground. He has never played the flamenco guitar.

Acknowledgements

Thanks, to:

Steve Annandale ▪ Professor Tony Bates ▪ Peter Charlton ▪ Bill Davies ▪ Isabelle Fournier ▪ Gill Fowler ▪ Andrew Gibbons ▪ Adrian Kirkwood ▪ Hugh Lloyd-Jones ▪ Steve Morris ▪ Peter Purdom ▪ Simon Shaw ▪ Paul Simpson ▪ Julie Vance

. . . for reading and commenting on the drafts.

Absolute beginning:

Learning can make the difference

This book is about *continuous* learning. It is about the learning that takes place every hour and every day of your waking life.

We believe that learning is a natural process. As human beings we share a uniquely rich capacity to learn. A dynamic economy and democratic society demand informed and questioning individuals who relish the challenge of learning. Today this power of learning is at a premium. This book will help you to meet this long-term challenge by learning and working more creatively and effectively.

This book will help you to learn and work more creatively and effectively.

Making a difference

We wanted to write this book because we are convinced that managers and professionals can become more aware of how they learn and can use this awareness to become more powerful – as learners and as individuals.

To achieve this you need to *know* about learning – to understand the process that has played the major part in making you what you are, influencing how you relate with other people, and determining what you have achieved and what you will be able to achieve in the future. There has been so much work and writing on this topic but very few books which offer a practical overview. We wanted to gather together the messages that we believe are central to learning and empowerment for individuals, organisations and society in the 21st century:

- *Learning can make a difference to you.* A dynamic approach to learning can help you to make the maximum possible contribution to your work, your family and any other activity that matters in your life. And learning can make a difference because it can and should be a real source of joy, excitement and satisfaction.

- *Learning can make a difference to your organisation.* In today's rapidly changing and competitive climate, learning is the only way that any organisation can make the most of their most precious and irreplaceable resource – the people who provide creativity, energy and the capacity to change.

- *Learning can make a difference to society as a whole.* Individual and collective learning offers the only chance for us to move forward together, learning from the mistakes of the past and creating a safer, fairer yet more exciting future.

Where's the evidence?

Of course today's shops are full of books that claim to help you become a better manager. Too many of these books are crammed with sound bites that signify very little – blind assertions with little valid evidence to back them up. Becoming a powerful learner will take you beyond the sound bite – you will learn to look beneath the surface and judge whether or not something is helpful to you.

This book is grounded in our own research and experience, in the research of other people and in the ideas of some of the most influential thinkers about learning – our 'learning gurus' who you will meet in Chapter 1. None of which means that we expect you to agree with everything we say – we expect you to question and look critically at what you read – but at least you will know where our ideas come from, and this will help you to judge how much weight you should give them.

This book is for you if . . .

The book will be relevant to anyone who needs to learn for or at work. We recognise that, in today's economy, we are all managers – of our own work and probably that of others; that we all work to professional standards; and that we are all knowledge workers. This book is for you whether you see yourself as a manager, a knowledge worker or a professional, and it will help you in all three aspects of your work.

The book will also be highly relevant if you are studying, or considering studying, a formal learning programme such as an MBA or a professional qualification.

Outcomes

Here are some of the things you will gain from reading this book:

Understanding how we learn	see Chapter 1
Identifying your learning needs	see Chapter 2
Identifying opportunities for learning	see Chapter 2
Diagnosing how you learn	see Chapter 3
Choosing tools to help you learn	see Chapter 5
Quantifying what you learn	see Chapter 6
Questioning the way things are	see Chapter 8
Communicating what you have learned	see Chapter 11
Understanding the information explosion	see Chapter 12

1

To learn is human

It's learning that makes my work so interesting. Everyone I
see is a different person and I have to treat them as an
individual, and find out what is special about them. I have
to learn all the time – both from experience, and keeping
up-to-date with new theories and methods.

These comments happen to have been made by a physiotherapist – but
they could just as easily have come from one of the many other managers
we meet in the course of our work. Learning is now high on many agen-
das. The purpose of this book is to help you improve your performance
in this vital area so that you can bring a dynamic, informed and questioning approach to every aspect of your work – and, indeed, every other
area of your life.

   This chapter sets the scene by looking at why learning and development has become one of today's burning issues, recognising that the
arguments in favour of learning range from the political and economic to
the intensely personal. We introduce our own beliefs and assumptions
about learning. And we also take a look at the 'theory' of learning, arguing that as human beings we all learn all of the time and introducing a
selection of the writers whose ideas you will find discussed and examined throughout the rest of this book.

   So this chapter explores:

- What is the good of learning? – the three Es: economy, empowerment and enjoyment.

- Our learning values – our own views about what learning involves and why it is so important.

- Our learning gurus – ten writers and thinkers who have been especially influential for us, and whose work we will refer to throughout the book.

What is the good of learning?

The basic message of this book is very simple. It is that today success as a manager depends not so much on what you already know but on how much, how quickly and how effectively you can learn.

We are certainly not alone in holding the opinion that learning is a 'good thing': to a large extent this has become an item of conventional wisdom. Our work with individuals, companies and government departments shows us, however, that people's belief in the power of learning may mask contrasting goals and objectives. When we have asked the question 'Why is lifelong learning important?', we have been given a wide variety of overlapping but by no means identical replies. Generally they fall into three categories:

- **Economy**. You need to learn – and to learn well – to be employable. And organisations need to be good at learning if they are to remain competitive.

- **Empowerment**. Learning can help you to unlock your full potential and play a more active part in shaping your own life.

- **Enjoyment**. Learning is fun and a willingness to learn allows you to gain pleasure and enjoyment from more of the things that you do.

These 'three Es' – economy, empowerment and enjoyment – provide a modern equivalent to the more traditional 'three Rs' of primary school education: reading, 'riting and 'rithmatic. Here are some examples of each of the three Es in action.

Economy

The first E is for economy. We believe that learning is crucial to survival in today's fast changing world – both for individuals and for organisations. Is there any evidence for this? Well, during the early and mid-1990s there was an economic slow-down in most of the world's major economies. As in the late 1970s and early 1980s many companies tightened their belts.

However, there was a difference this time round – in a refreshing number of instances training budgets were not the first casualties. Faced with an acid test, it seems that an increasing number of senior managers had recognised the value of learning. They had accepted that the firms which continued to invest in professional and personal development were often the quickest to take advantage when the financial climate became more favourable.

So the economic justification for lifelong learning centres around competitiveness. In a dynamic economy, where change is the norm, the individuals and organisations which thrive and prosper will be those which are able to change and to keep at least one step ahead of any developments which come along.

Tom Peters stresses just how important this is for individuals. Coining the idea that each of us today needs a 'personal brand', Peters comments that:

The good news – and it is largely good news – is that everyone has a chance to stand out. Everyone has a chance to learn, improve and build up their skills.

The Brand Called You (Peters, 1999)

And here is an example of a firm which accepts this argument – one of the five most widely recognised brand names in the world[1].

---

[1] According to an annual Global Survey conducted by the Sterling Group.

Coca-Cola Enterprises' SkillStart Programme

In 1996 Coca-Cola Enterprises Ltd, following their earlier success with a sponsored degree programme in their commercial department, decided to look in other areas of the business for opportunities to combine work-based training with education through distance learning. One area with clear potential was Operations. The business is highly seasonal, with demand for soft drinks varying with the weather. Given the fickle nature of the British summertime, demand can be unpredictable. Traditionally, in order to meet this demand the company has employed large numbers of temporary staff during the peak seasons. The employment of temporary staff incurred several costs – in particular the costs of recruitment and training. Temporary staff were often released in the quieter periods, only for the company to have to re-recruit and train a few weeks later.

The company was also concerned about the issues faced by young people trying to obtain employment. Many could not get jobs because they lacked experience but were unable to get the experience without a job.

The answer to these problems lay with the development of the company SkillStart Programme. Under this scheme, 18 to 23 year olds are recruited on a two-year contract, under which they receive a high quality education and training programme leading to a nationally recognised advanced GNVQ (General National Vocational Qualification) qualification.

During their time on the programme SkillStarters work in many areas of manufacturing and distribution, and make a real contribution to the output of the operation.

Coca-Cola Enterprises' investment in this programme is considerable. In addition to the salaries of the young people, the company have paid for the development of a suite of learning materials which allow the SkillStarters to learn and produce evidence of their achievements from each of their work roles. Coca-Cola Enterprises Ltd also funds the residential schools, assessment arrangements and support for workplace staff who act as mentors.

This investment in learning has clearly paid off. Attrition rates are significantly lower than the national average for full-time college-based courses and the GNVQ results have been outstanding – over a third of the first cohort of

SkillStarters achieved distinctions. An additional benefit to the company has been the successful recruitment of a high proportion of these young people into established operational positions.

It is useful to recognise that this economic emphasis on lifelong learning is endorsed both by commercial organisations and by national governments. Both rely on adaptable, creative people who are ready and willing to learn in order to meet the challenge of change and unpredictability.

The Key Skills Support Programme

During 1999 the UK government announced plans for a new key skills qualification – combining Communication, Application of Number and Information Technology – which would become available to all 16–18 year olds in government-funded education and training programmes, whether academic (advanced GCE), pre-vocational (GNVQ) or work-based (NVQ).

The government put £17 million of 'new' money into a three-year Key Skills Support Programme designed to underpin the introduction of this new qualification through a series of demonstration projects, support materials, conferences and workshops. Announcing this programme the government minister, Baroness Blackstone, justified the initiative purely in economic terms:

'For the nation to sustain healthy economic growth it is vital that many more young people develop these skills.' [2]

What is more, a third of this funding has been allocated to the roughly 10 per cent of young people involved in work-based education and training, underlining the value which policy makers place on workplace learning – where most lifelong learning takes place.

[2] Taken from a government press release dated 12 July 1999.

Empowerment

A person is at their best, their most fulfilled, when they are on the way to becoming what they are going to become.

The Money Game (Adam Smith)

By playing an active part in the learning process you can release more of your potential and gain greater personal satisfaction.

But while learning is important for economic reasons, this is just the start. Career-long learning is crucial to unlocking your true or hidden potential, so that you have the scope to develop your abilities to the full. The implication is that most of us have the chance to use only a limited proportion of our skills and abilities in our day-to-day working lives. By playing an active part in the learning process you can release more of your potential and gain greater personal satisfaction while making a fuller contribution to society.

Paulo Freire and empowerment in the third world

Perhaps the most influential of all advocates of learning for empowerment was the adult educator Paolo Freire. Working with illiterates in his native Brazil, Freire argued that true learning only takes place when we can each take active responsibility for our own development, and that the progress that results when this happens can be startling.

Teaching in the Brazil of the early 1960s, Freire was concerned with empowerment in a very real and immediate sense. To qualify to vote in national elections citizens were required to prove that they could read. Freire worked with the most disadvantaged groups in his society, helping them to learn to read so that they could play a full role in the political system. Freire, an avowed Marxist, was seen as a subversive and became an exile, moving first to Chile and later to the United States. It was this which allowed his work to become more widely known. Freire's focus on learning as empowerment has since influenced many practitioners, irrespective of their own political inclinations.

You can find out more about Freire's philosophy of learning in books like *Education: The Practice of Freedom* and *Pedagogy of the Oppressed*. Chapter 4 of this book looks at these ideas in more detail.

The empowerment case argues that you should have the opportunity to learn because it is right that you should release more of your potential. The following example shows how the design of one employer-based programme has been influenced by this perspective.

Empowerment at work – the Post Office First Steps Programme

A few years ago we were involved in the development of materials which supported an in-house management development programme. The pack opened with the following questions:

- *Are you fulfilling your potential?*
- *Do you feel you've achieved all you want in life?*
- *Does your job really stretch you?*
- *Do you think that you're in the right job – one which makes the most of your interests and abilities?*

This programme was developed by the Post Office at a time when they realised that relatively few of their female employees moved from first line jobs to management. The aim of the materials was to encourage women of all ages in the Post Office to take their 'first steps' into a managerial role. As the following statement shows, empowerment formed an important part of the rationale for this programme:

'In doing this, the programme acknowledges what many of us already know – that not just in the Post Office, but in many areas of life, women's skills and abilities are under-used and often unrecognised as an important and untapped resource.'

Enjoyment

Learning can be fun. Learning should be enjoyable.

How to Win as an Open Learner (Race, 1986)

If only more writers on the subject had Phil Race's attitude! We have a shelf-full of guides to self-study, all of which begin by encouraging the reader to think about why he or she might be starting a new course. And yet Phil's little booklet is the only one which mentions what we believe is one of the most important reasons to value learning – the fact that it might actually be fun; a source of happiness and entertainment rather than worry and frustration. Perhaps it is a hangover from the protestant work ethic, but there seems to be a reluctance to acknowledge the possibility that learning might actually bring a smile to the face.

Yet there is no doubt that learning can be enjoyable. At the end of a successful workshop it is not uncommon for participants to say that they have really enjoyed themselves and to link their enjoyment to the fact that they have learned something.

Learning we have enjoyed

We thought that it might be a good idea for us to share some of the learning experiences that have given us pleasure and enjoyment.

- I hated just about everything at school with one exception – I loved history. Why? Because I liked the topics, had good teachers and worked in a good group. But above all I enjoyed making links and exploring how our society today has been influenced by myriad events from the past.

- Learning to scuba-dive was great fun. Each session started with an hour in the pool followed by an hour in the classroom – there is a great deal of technical knowledge needed to dive safely. I think it was the combination of activity and theory that made the course really enjoyable. And of course there was the social side – meeting in the pub afterwards, holidays and trips – which also provided the chance to learn from more experienced divers.

Even though it was hard work, time-consuming and sometimes daunting I did enjoy studying for the master's degree I have recently completed. I found myself genuinely excited by the ideas and literature I was introduced to and could sometimes feel quite 'high' as a result! Having learnt a lot of the skills I use at work on the job, I liked the feeling of being a student again with lecturers and tutors there to support and help me.

Recently I was involved in a series of events to train inspectors of workplace training. Because this was a completely new development the team included two kinds of people. Some, like myself, were brought in because we were thought to know something about workplace learning, others had extensive experience of inspection in colleges. To begin with we sat on opposite sides of the table and were quite suspicious of each others' credentials, but one of the great pleasures of the project was the way the two groups learned from each other. I really enjoyed getting to know these people – who are now my friends – and coming to understand how they went about their work.

No learning please – we're qualified!

In this book we shall be drawing on our practical experiences and on a wide range of theory and research. All of these sources of information include reminders that there are people – including experienced managers – who might question the three Es. The following example shows how, a few years ago, we had a stark reminder of this when we experienced one of the least successful days in our professional careers.

A bad day at work . . .

One morning during the early 1990s, two of us set off to one of the country's leading manufacturing and engineering companies. It is important to stress that this was – and remains – a company which places a major emphasis on the importance of personal and professional development.

Each autumn the company recruits about 100 new graduates straight from university as the potential executives and project leaders of the future. They join a programme through which they experience not only their 'own' department – design, engineering, human resources and so on – but also other parts of the operation so that they can get a clear picture of how the firm operates.

Our task was to run a workshop in which we encouraged them to keep a formal record of their learning and achievements during their first few months. Senior personnel staff believed that this might help the graduates to learn more from their initial orientation period.

We introduced the learning record to them, tried hard to explain how it might help them both now and in the future and split them into groups to discuss how they might use it. Their response was virtually unanimous: quite simply they did not want to know. They did not believe that they could gain any benefit from recording their experiences and progress. When, at the end of the day we asked them to fill in a form to indicate whether or not they would be willing to take part in the trial of the record, they all turned the offer down. What is more, several of the forms they returned were downright abusive.

Once we had allowed a few days for the dust to settle, we were able to look back at the event and learn from it. It was clear from the reactions of the graduate entrants that the company had chosen the wrong point in their careers at which to introduce the idea of reflective learning. Many of these young people were justly proud of what they had recently achieved. They had all just left university with good degree results and they had landed attractive jobs with a famous and internationally respected company. After a very long period in formal education they were now making their way as newly fledged professionals. They had come to a point where they wanted to rest on their laurels and to get credit for what they had already achieved rather than to plan their route ahead.

Fortunately, this experience has been a relatively rare one in our working lives – indeed when we ran a similar event with another group of (non-graduate) young people in the same company, it went much better. The graduates were, however, a highly talented group of people who had yet to be convinced that learning and development should be one of their professional priorities. We would not say that they were 'wrong' to take the view that they did. Rather we suspect that their experience of formal education had not given them a full view of the learning process.

Learning is not something that can be switched on and off – and it is certainly not something that is confined to the classroom or lecture theatre. On the contrary, it is as much a basic human function as sleeping or breathing.

Our learning values

The three Es show why learning should be treated as a priority. But in introducing this topic as a whole it is also important to examine what research and theory have to say about the nature of the learning process itself.

We begin with four basic assumptions which have important implications for the role of learning in professional life and for an understanding of the most effective approaches to learning. Our four assumptions are:

- **Learning is a continuous process** – we all learn all the time.

- **Learning is an active process** – it is something that we do rather than something that is done to us.

- **Learning is something that we are good at** – we all have an enormous capacity to learn.

- **Learning is important** – the way that we approach learning has major implications for each of us as individuals and for the future of our society.

Over the next few pages we shall examine each of these assumptions in more detail. The first assumption is, however, the most important: the other three follow on from it logically. Essentially, this assumption is that learning happens every minute of the day.

Learning is a continuous process

The Campaign for Learning also works from the assumption that learning is a natural, everyday experience. Here is an extract from their working definition of the learning process:

Learning is a process of active engagement with experience. It is what people do when they want to make sense of the world.

Working to Create an Appetite for Learning (Campaign for Learning, 1998)

The Campaign for Learning

Originally set up by the Royal Society for the Arts (RSA) during 1995, this high profile campaign starts from a vision of:

'An inclusive society, in which learning is valued, understood, wanted and widely available to everyone. A world in which everyone is seen as having the potential to learn.'

Its goal is to:

. . . *'create an appetite for learning in individuals that will sustain them for life.'*

The Campaign promotes lifelong learning through a wide range of publications, project partnerships and nationwide events. These events have included a 'learning at work' day and a 'family learning weekend'. The Campaign has won the active support of a broad spectrum of organisations, from major corporations such as British Airways, Microsoft and Sainsbury's to voluntary and government bodies including the Department for Education and Employment (DfEE).

Clearly the Campaign's definition is closely in line with our own basic assumptions – but in our view it does not go far enough in establishing the continuous nature of learning. We would take issue with the implication that individuals have some measure of choice over whether or not they learn. There is a considerable body of literature which, like the Campaign for Learning, links the process of learning with the need to make sense of the outside world. The theorists who have considered this topic, however, see this as a process that goes on throughout our waking lives.

We take as our starting point the theories offered by two of the most influential psychologists of the last 50 years: the American George Kelly and the Swiss Jean Piaget.

Testing assumptions . . .

In his book *The Psychology of Personal Constructs* George Kelly offered the model of 'man the scientist'. Kelly's argument was that our actions are shaped by the way that we each see and interpret the world. He rejected the idea that human beings simply react passively to what is going on around them. Instead, Kelly argued that we use our experience to build up a series of 'constructs' which help us to structure the way that we see what happens around us and to make predictions about what will happen next. In his view these constructs have much in common with the theories and hypotheses that scientists use to govern their research. Our personal constructs are not as formal or systematic as scientific theories — indeed we may not always be able to state our constructs in words — but, much like a scientist, we do constantly test them by acting as if they were true.

To give an example, when I meet a new person the way that I approach him or her is influenced by an interconnecting set of constructs that I have built up over the years. On first sight I might see the person as a tall, thin woman, rather than a short, plump man. If we strike up a conversation different constructs will come into play. I might, for instance, start to see my new acquaintance as articulate, humorous and interesting rather than tongue-tied, dull and boring. And I will start to make assumptions about her other characteristics. So, if she tells me that she is a great admirer of Nelson Mandela I might start to see her as 'progressive' and 'liberal' and make some subconscious predictions about her views on other subjects — personally I might assume that she has some interest in human rights issues and in politics in general.

Crucially, Kelly argued that our personal constructs are not set in concrete; they are open to change and refinement. Like a scientist I will sometimes come across 'data' which do not fit my theories — for instance someone who admires Nelson Mandela but takes no interest at all in human rights issues. As a result I will, consciously or unconsciously, make changes to my construct system. In other words, by constantly acting on the basis of past experience, I am testing out my assumptions and therefore learning all the time.

. . . through assimilation and accommodation

Piaget's theory of cognitive development in the child is having profound effects on teaching methods. Piaget and Kelly have much in common including the conviction that human beings should be regarded as 'thinkers' rather than 'organisms' or 'computers' or entirely bound by their 'unconscious dynamics'. Both argued that if we listen credulously to what people, child or adult, say, then we may start to understand why they approach life in the way that they do.

Inquiring Man (Bannister and Fransella, 1971)

Piaget is famous for arguing that children go though a sequence of intellectual stages – so that a five-year-old thinks and acts in a way that is characteristically different from an eight-year-old and different again from a thirteen-year-old. The exact details of these stages have become a matter for debate, but this is not the purpose of introducing Piaget into the present discussion. Instead, we are interested in his view of the learning process.

Piaget argued (see Piaget and Inhelder, 1969) that an individual's actions are organised into a series of what he calls *schemata* which we use routinely to solve a variety of problems. Piaget's schemata have some clear similarities with Kelly's notion of personal constructs: both are concerned with our tendency to categorise and interpret. Piaget suggested that when faced with a new situation we have two options open to us: assimilation or accommodation.

■   *Assimilation* happens when we handle a new situation by applying an existing schema. We make the new situation fit with our existing world view.

■ *Accommodation* takes place when we make adjustments to our routine schemata to cope with something new. In these cases our existing world view is modified to fit in with the new situation.

So, to return to the earlier example, if my conversation with my new acquaintance led me to question my assumption that admirers of Nelson Mandela are necessarily concerned with human rights issues this would, in Piaget's terms, be an example of my accommodating my views in the light of experience.

For Piaget learning hinges on the resolution of the tension between assimilation and accommodation – the conflict between using old responses in new situations and acquiring new ones, or updating old ones, to cope with change. For both Piaget and Kelly, and for many other researchers, this is a continuous process: there is never a time when we are not learning.

In Chapter 2 we will explore what this means in practice – and Chapter 6 looks at how you can get better at learning continuously.

Learning is an active process. . .

The primary task of the teacher is to *permit* the student to learn, to feed his or her own curiosity.

Freedom to Learn for the 80's (Rogers, 1983)

Throughout this book the focus is on learning rather than teaching. This distinction is significant and goes beyond semantics. It puts the emphasis on the active role of the learner. This contrasts with the 'traditional' model where it was the teacher or trainer who had an active part to play in the education process. He or she handed over knowledge to the student or demonstrated particular skills or techniques. The student, by contrast, was a passive recipient; an 'empty vessel' to be filled with new insights and understanding by somebody else blessed with more knowledge, experience and status.

Of course this is a caricature – the 'traditional model' was never a very accurate picture of how learning actually takes place. The most effective teachers and trainers have always recognised that there are

The best teacher in the world cannot make you learn – you have an active part to play and are largely responsible for the progress that you make.

severe limits on what they can achieve on their own. The best teacher in the world cannot make you learn – you have an active part to play and are largely responsible for the progress that you make.

There is a close relationship between the assumption that learning is an active process and learning as empowerment. Passive learning situations – the endlessly boring lecture, the hard to follow demonstration – fail because they do not engage and involve the learner. Whenever a lecturer or instructor misses an opportunity to invite questions or to ask you to try something for yourself he or she is failing to exploit your power as a learner. The effect is, literally, *de*-powering.

. . . and we can be pretty good at it!

What is it that defines a human being? Many writers have tried to answer this question, striving to find characteristics – our capacity for language, our level of consciousness or awareness, our ability to tell right from wrong, and so on – which distinguish us from other animals in terms of our mental abilities and which single us out even from the apes with whom we share many physical characteristics.

None of these attempts has ever been wholly convincing. To give an example, at one time the argument that we have unique linguistic powers seemed quite promising – but then researchers found that chimpanzees could learn and routinely use hundreds of words from the American Sign Language for the Deaf. Nevertheless, there do seem to be certain activities that human beings are particularly, if not uniquely, good at. Our assumption is that our talent for learning is one of the clearest examples.

Compared with virtually any other species – including the great apes – human beings are unusually helpless when they are born. Newborn lambs are able to get around on their own within a matter of minutes, but it is years before a human being can begin to fend for him- or herself. Quite simply the human baby faces a steeper and longer learning curve. It seems that rather less is programmed in at birth and that we depend for our survival and success on a relatively greater capacity to learn. The result is a species which is distributed right across the globe and which has had a major, and in many ways dangerous, impact on the environment as a whole. Human beings, all human beings, are very good at learning. This 'human power' has given us our culture, a capacity to acquire knowledge and to share it not just with the people that we meet but with future generations.

Harré and Secord – let's think of people as human beings

Harré and Secord's 1972 book *The Explanation of Social Behaviour* was deliberately controversial. It fired a broadside at many of the assumptions that had been built up by experimental psychologists. Based at Oxford University, Romano Harré was not himself a psychologist but an eminent philosopher and historian of science. This put him, and his colleague P. F. Secord (himself a distinguished American social psychologist), in a unique position from which they could argue that many psychologists had a mistaken and outdated view of how research is carried out in the more 'advanced' sciences, such as physics, chemistry and biology.

In particular, they took issue with the 'behaviourist' tradition. This is still highly influential and argues that psychologists should focus exclusively on what can be observed by a third person, paying little attention to what the subjects of their experiments have to say about their actions and experiences. Harré and Secord maintained that this 'self-denying ordinance' had no justification in scientific methods as practised in other disciplines and was flawed because it wasted a rich and powerful source of data. Instead, they argued, a truly scientific approach would start from what we already know and understand from our everyday experience of human life and, in their words, 'treat people as if they were human beings'.

Harré and Secord themselves hardly use the word 'learning' in their book, but their 'anthropomorphic model of man' does hinge on two key concepts which have considerable relevance to our own interpretation of the learning process.

■ *Human powers.* For Harré and Secord human powers are a set of general capabilities – notably the power of language – which make us characteristically human. Our own view is that the 'power of learning' is one of the most crucial of all these capabilities. Of course other animals share this power but it is uniquely developed amongst human beings – we all have tremendous potential as learners.

■ *Social episodes.* Harré and Secord argued that it is helpful to see human behaviour in terms of 'episodes'. According to them an episode is an event or series of events which has meaning and coherence to the individuals involved. Some episodes, say a quick coffee with a colleague, may last only a matter of minutes. Others – say a long-term management project – may consist of a sequence of interconnected events over a period of months or years. We shall see in Chapter 6 that it can often be useful to think in terms of 'learning episodes' when reflecting on and learning from our experiences. One of the characteristics of professional, as opposed to shop-floor, life is that the most significant learning episodes tend to consist of a larger number of linked events.

One other assumption about our capabilities as learners should be teased out at this point. This is that one of the most important human powers is the ability to 'learn to learn'. In other words, although we all have the potential to be powerful learners, we can also all learn to become better learners. Chapter 5, in particular, will help you to hone your skills in this area.

Learning matters

Our fourth assumption about the learning process has, in effect, already been stated several times in this chapter. It is that learning is a vital area of performance for today's professional and, indeed, for today's citizen. Clearly learning has always been important but there are two factors at work today which imply that effective learning will continue to gain even greater significance:

■ *The pace of change.* Individual learning and organisational change are inextricably connected. The ability of managers and professionals to learn quickly and effectively is probably the most important factor determining the capacity of an organisation – or an economy – to cope with new challenges. All the indications are that these challenges will continue to come along at a rate which was difficult to imagine even as recently as the 1960s.

■ *The information explosion.* A theme that we shall return to several times during this book is the fact that there is a quite unprecedented amount of information available to today's manager and professional. This is not simply the result of developments such as email and the World Wide Web which mean that information can be shared more quickly but also the fact that more research is being carried out than ever before. Today's professional must keep up-to-date with this expanding and changing knowledge base. This means more than merely assimilating new facts. We must also be prepared to accommodate new concepts – new ways of looking at our specialist areas and new skills and techniques which were not available when we went through our initial training.

The position of medical doctors in general practice provides a good example of both of these factors in action. Medical research is a vast, international undertaking. Every year there are thousands of researchers producing tens of thousands of journal articles, many of which could have some practical implications for the day-to-day work of the average GP. Doctors need both to keep up-to-date with this new knowledge and make sure they genuinely understand the implications that it has for their practice, if they are to continue to provide the highest quality service to their patients – in the most cost-effective way possible.

We will look at the implications of the information explosion in later chapters.

Our learning gurus

Having shared our assumptions about the learning process, it also makes sense to highlight the writers and researchers who have most influenced our approach. So here, in alphabetical order, is our own 'top ten' list of the authors who have offered ideas and insights which are discussed and critically examined in the rest of this book.

- **Patricia Benner**. A nurse researcher, Benner's classic book *From Novice to Expert* provided some valuable insights into how professionals develop expertise in their field – insights that are equally valuable for managers and professionals.

- **Paulo Freire**. A practising adult educator who stressed the relevance of learning to involvement in the political process, Freire also highlighted the need to work from the perspective of the learner rather than the preconceptions of the teacher.

- **John Holt**. Holt wrote two thought provoking books *How Children Fail* and *How Children Learn* based on his daily experiences as a primary teacher in New York. He argued, quite persuasively, that much traditional teaching practice produces a fear of failure amongst students and prevents them from developing and exploiting their powers as learners.

- **Rosabeth Moss Kanter**. In books such as *When Giants Learn to Dance* Moss Kanter has highlighted the importance of continuous professional development in meeting the challenge of change. Along with writers like Tom Peters, Richard Schonberger and W. Edwards Deming, she played a major role in the rise of the TQM (Total Quality Management) movement.

- **George Kelly**. In his book *The Psychology of Personal Constructs* Kelly argued that people are constantly interpreting and reinterpreting their environment so that they can anticipate future events through their actions. He also argued that questions are more important than answers.

David Kolb. Drawing heavily on the work of Kurt Lewin and Jean Piaget, Kolb has provided one of the most rigorous theoretical analyses of the factors which make for effective learning in adulthood.

Jean Piaget. As part of an attempt to understand the nature of human knowledge, Piaget presented learning as a continuous process of assimilation and accommodation through which we refine and develop our 'schemata'.

Carl Rogers. A highly influential figure in counselling psychology – he invented the concept of client-centred counselling – in his later career Rogers went on to champion the importance of student-centred learning. He highlighted the concept of 'responsible freedom' as a way of describing effective independent learning.

Donald Schön. Schön is one of the most influential writers on the process of learning from experience through reflection. His studies of professionals at work have helped us to understand how people respond to often highly complex and challenging problems.

B. F. Skinner. A dedicated experimental psychologist, Skinner is, in many ways, the 'odd one out' in this list in that he took a strictly behaviourist approach, arguing that learning can be understood entirely in terms of events that take place within the environment. For us, however, the value of his ideas lies in the emphasis he placed on the importance of feedback in reinforcing the learning process.

Skinner: The Science of Learning and the Art of Teaching

For someone who spent most of his working life studying rats who had learned to press levers Skinner was an extraordinarily controversial figure. In books like *Beyond Freedom and Dignity* and his novel *Walden Two* he seemed almost to court notoriety with views calculated to challenge our basic assumptions about human nature and how society should operate. In *Walden Two*, for example, he imagined an 'ideal' society governed not by elected politicians but by behavioural scientists who managed a 'token economy' of rewards and punishments.

Today these books have become historical curios; nobody takes Skinner's highly idiosyncratic politics too seriously. But his ideas have influenced the development of open learning materials and computer-aided learning. In his classic paper 'The Science of Learning and the Art of Teaching' Skinner castigated schools for failing to provide enough feedback (or 'reinforcement' to use Skinner's own term) and for often allowing big delays between a student handing in work and finding our what mark he or she had received. He advocated the use of 'teaching machines' which could give immediate feedback – this has been a major influence on the use of computers in schools. His argument was that this would allow their teacher to concentrate on more important things:

'. . . intellectual, cultural and emotional contact of that distinctive sort which testify to her status as a human being.'

It is important to stress that there are significant contrasts in the ways that these different writers present the learning process. We imagine, for example, that Paulo Freire might have been quite amused at the suggestion that his ideas have much in common with those of Skinner – who is usually thought of as a right wing, authoritarian writer. There are, however, a number of recurring themes which apply to many, if not all, of them and which are central to the ideas presented in later chapters:

- In each case the focus is on learning rather than teaching; throughout this book the emphasis is on how you can play a full and active part in shaping and managing your own development.

- Many of these writers – notably Benner, Moss Kanter and Schön – are concerned with the concept of 'professionalism'; they stress the importance of reflecting critically on accepted practices.

- There is an ethical, even political, dimension to the ideas put forward by the majority of these writers. They see the learning process as profoundly important, the key to a 'better' future, however defined.

We do not wholly endorse the ideas of any of these writers. Rather their value lies in the questions that they pose, and, as we shall see in Chapter 8, asking the right questions is one of the most important characteristics of an effective learner.

2 A world of opportunities

It will be clear from Chapter 1 that we do not see learning as something restricted to schools and colleges. We believe learning happens throughout our lives, as a natural and integrated part of our personal growth and our search for rewarding and satisfying lives.

This can, however, make learning harder to grasp. If learning happens all the time, how do you recognise it when it happens? This chapter develops these issues in greater detail. It explores the idea that learning is about making the most of the opportunities you encounter, recognising these when they occur, and selecting those that will most help you to develop.

The chapter explores:

▨ The richest opportunity of all? – how the workplace provides a rich learning environment with a blend of planned and incidental learning opportunities.

▨ A lifeline for learning – using the learning lifeline to examine past, present and future learning and identifying your learning needs.

▨ Uncovering your motives for learning – learning is most successful when it is something we want to do. So it is important to be able to identify positive reasons for learning, and to turn these into goals to direct and support your own progress.

▨ Breaking down the barricades – achieving your goals is not always easy. We all meet barriers that can stop us making the most of our learning. It is vital to recognise these, and to find ways of overcoming them.

The richest opportunity of all?

Chapter 1 introduced our basic assumptions – in particular, our view that learning is both a continuous and active process. We believe that learning happens all the time, as a result of trying things out, doing things, talking to other people or working in a team. We believe that learning happens everywhere – not just in the classroom, but at work and leisure and in our personal, family and social lives. And we believe that we are the architects of our own learning; while other people – teachers, trainers and so forth – can support and guide us, only we, ourselves, can actually 'do' the learning.

Of course these ideas are not new. Writing in 1933, John Dewey suggested that learning is a process that goes on as long as life continues. And David Kolb, whose ideas about experiential learning were influenced by Dewey, describes learning as 'a continuous process grounded in experience':

This concept of learning is much broader than that commonly associated with the school classroom. It occurs in all human settings, from schools to the workplace, from the research laboratory to the management board room, in personal relationships and the aisles of the local grocery. It encompasses all life stages, from childhood to adolescence, to middle and old age

Experiential Learning (Kolb, 1984)

Indeed, some writers question whether schools are actually good places to learn in at all. Ivan Illich, in his radical critique of education, *Deschooling Society*, questions the role of schools in helping people to learn. He argues that much of the money spent in the United States – and elsewhere – on formal education is wasted and calls on politicians to 'disestablish school' and to 'deschool society'.

We would not go this far ourselves. We believe that, for all the defects of formal education and training, much valuable learning does take place in schools, colleges, universities and training rooms, and that most teachers and trainers are highly committed to helping people to learn. However, the focus of this book is not on formal education and training – it is on the learning that, in Illich's words, 'seems to happen casually and as a by-product of some other activity defined as work or leisure'. Above all, in this chapter we will explore the importance of the workplace as a learning environment.

The workplace is a great place to learn

Over the last ten years we have carried out a number of research projects which have looked at the way people learn at work. We have talked to people in a wide range of contexts – from motor manufacturers to biscuit bakers, from soft drink producers to bank managers, and from healthcare professionals to sheep farmers. Again and again people have told us that the workplace is a great place to learn.

Learning on a dairy farm

John met the owner of a dairy farm to discuss his experiences of learning. His first reaction was to describe his time at agricultural college. However, as we started to discuss in greater detail the critical parts of his job – the things that could make the difference between life and death for his herd such as illness and problem calvings – a different picture emerged. His most important learning had in fact taken place on the farm, as a result of his experiences and observations of animal behaviour. And he felt it had taken him several years to get to know cows well enough to deal with the most challenging problems he faces.

This experience is repeated in many other contexts. One trainer at a major manufacturer introduces the principles behind work-based learning to experienced trainers with this invitation:

Hands up anyone who did an apprenticeship. Now, keep your hands up if you were able to do the job when you had finished your apprenticeship.

We believe that this growing awareness of the value of the workplace for learning marks one of the most important shifts in vocational education over recent years. During the 1970s in particular, there was a concern that if people learnt by 'sitting by Nellie' then they risked picking up bad practices. Such concerns promoted the belief that formal, off-job training offered a safer route for getting the company message across.

Any commitment to empowering learners must challenge this view – we believe that the workplace offers a rich environment for learning, provided that people have the support they need, when they need it.

Planned and incidental learning opportunities

It is important to recognise that workplace learning is rather different from formal education and training. As one HR manager told us:

Learning in the workplace is about seizing opportunities, whenever and wherever they arise.

It's about making the most of the largely haphazard and unplanned succession of learning opportunities which take place every day.

The crucial word here is 'opportunities'. Learning in the workplace is about seizing opportunities, whenever and wherever they arise. They could include:

- taking on a new managerial responsibility

- leading a new team

- delegating work to other people

- making mistakes

- something unexpected

- things that go wrong

- things that go right

- feedback from a colleague

- visiting another site, and so on.

Our research work, leading up to the publication *Becoming Competent* (Knasel and Meed, 1994), suggested an important distinction here:

■ Many of these opportunities for learning will be *incidental* – where you learn from an unanticipated experience at work. Chapter 6 looks more closely at how you can learn from experience through the process of reflection.

■ However, there is also scope to influence your learning in practice, and to create *planned* opportunities for learning. Spending time thinking in advance about what you may learn at work can help you to make the most of these opportunities.

Making the most of appraisal

One of the best ways of creating planned opportunities for learning is appraisal. You can use your own appraisals to identify:

■ What do you need to learn?

■ What new challenges could you take on?

■ Who can help you to learn?

■ Who can you learn with?

The Internet as a learning opportunity

The Internet now offers some exciting opportunities for learning. You can use the web to obtain information in a wide range of ways, including:

■ Using search engines such as Excite, Yahoo!, Lycos or Infoseek to look up key words central to what you wish to learn.

■ Following links from one web site to another – 'surfing' the web.

■ Consulting the web pages of broadcasters and newspapers.

In addition, there are specific web sites that are likely to be essentials for any learner. These include:

▷

Libraries on the web. Increasingly, libraries are making their catalogues available on the web. For example, you can consult the British Library catalogue on http://opac97.bl.uk/. You can also order reprints of articles or chapters from books from the British Library Document Supply Centre using their ARTEmail service – Automatic Request Transmission by Electronic Mail. Find out more on http://www.bl.uk.

Journals on the web. Most leading professional and management journals now have a web presence. For example, the *Harvard Business Review*, a leading source of research and writing about management, can be contacted on http://www.hbsp.harvard.edu/products/hbr. You can look up the content of different editions and even order offprints on-line.

Professional organisations. There are web sites for many professional organisations and awarding bodies who offer qualifications.

Educational institutions. You can compare the programmes, services and costs of different colleges, universities etc. by visiting their web sites. And, increasingly, educational institutions are using the Internet as a means of communication between students on the same course.

Sites about learning. There is also an increasing range of sites about learning. Contact the web site for this book for some more links.

Accessing the Internet is straightforward these days – most modern home computers come with a built-in modem, and there is a wide range of 'Internet providers', many of whom now offer free Internet access.

A lifeline for learning

If learning involves creating planned learning opportunities as well as grasping incidental learning opportunities when they arise, then to understand your own learning you need to be able to look critically at your past, present and future learning. In the process you can become clearer about where, when and how you learn best, and identify what you need to learn. One way of doing this is to use the idea of the learning lifeline (see Figure 2.1). The learning lifeline draws on the ideas of autobiographical learning described by Powell.

The learning lifeline

Examining the learning lifeline involves three stages:

■ Reflecting on past learning.

■ Anticipating future learning.

■ Exploring the present.

It can be done in several ways:

■ By writing about your experiences and expectations – past, present and future – of learning.

■ By describing and discussing your experiences and expectations with other people.

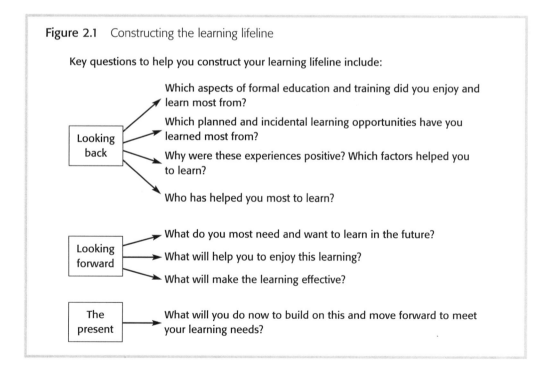

Figure 2.1   Constructing the learning lifeline

Key questions to help you construct your learning lifeline include:

Looking back
- Which aspects of formal education and training did you enjoy and learn most from?
- Which planned and incidental learning opportunities have you learned most from?
- Why were these experiences positive? Which factors helped you to learn?
- Who has helped you most to learn?

Looking forward
- What do you most need and want to learn in the future?
- What will help you to enjoy this learning?
- What will make the learning effective?

The present
- What will you do now to build on this and move forward to meet your learning needs?

By drawing maps or diagrams that show your most important learning experiences.

Your learning lifeline should include both your experiences of formal education and training, and the range of planned and incidental learning opportunities you have encountered in practice. Your learning lifeline will also show how your orientation to learning may have changed and varied over time.

Identifying your learning needs

The learning lifeline highlights the importance of identifying what you need to learn. But with things changing so fast, how can you be clear about what your most important learning needs are? You really need to carry out an audit of your learning needs.

Auditing your learning needs

Begin by thinking about your work as it currently is:

- What would you like to learn more about?
- Which parts of your work do you find most difficult?
- Which kinds of work do you not get involved in because you lack the necessary skills, knowledge or experience?

Then take a look at the changing world of work:

- What has changed in your line of work over the last five years?
- What might change over the next five years?
- What new skills and knowledge will you need to meet these challenges?

Then think longer term:

- What would you most like to be doing in five years' time? Ten years' time?
- What new activities might you be involved in?
- What extra skills and knowledge will you need to do this?

Your learning lifeline is also the starting point for:

- Exploring your reasons for learning.

- Identifying and overcoming barriers to learning.

The rest of this chapter will explore these issues in greater detail.

Uncovering your motives for learning

You have started to think about what you need to learn. Your reasons for learning may be to do with work – whether developing within your own job or organisation, or developing yourself for future work. They may be academic – for example, working towards a degree, MBA or other qualification. Or they may be more personal or social – for example, learning an instrument or a new language.

Any decision to learn in a conscious way will be influenced by at least one of the three Es introduced in Chapter 1: economy, empowerment and enjoyment. For example, while learning team leadership skills may be driven primarily by economy and empowerment, learning Tai Chi may be driven principally by enjoyment with little economic value.

Having clear reasons for learning is extremely important. They help you to set realistic and meaningful goals. You can also refer back to them if at any point you start to find learning difficult. In contrast, if you are not clear why you are learning something, it is much harder to remain focused on it.

Your reasons for learning will also have an important impact on whether you enjoy learning, whether you are able to stick at it, and whether the learning is effective. How exactly this will work for you will depend on your own preferences and approaches to learning. However, it is possible to distinguish between:

- Reactive and proactive reasons for learning.

- Extrinsic and intrinsic reasons for learning.

Reactive and proactive reasons for learning

People may approach learning for both reactive and proactive reasons:

- **Reactive** reasons for learning will involve responding to events. Examples could include being sent on a training course by your boss, or feeling driven to develop new skills in order to respond to organisational change, new technological developments or even the threat of redundancy.

- **Proactive** reasons for learning involve taking steps to anticipate events – looking ahead and planning what you will need to learn to stay on top of your work, to achieve your career goals and to keep up-to-date with developments.

Any decision to learn something is likely to involve both proactive and reactive reasons. However, if you take a proactive decision to learn something you are more likely to feel a sense of ownership, commitment and control. If, on the other hand, the predominant reasons are reactive you are more likely to feel pressured, coerced and out of control.

Extrinsic and intrinsic reasons for learning

In her book *Adults Learning* Jenny Rogers argues that there are two types of factor that may encourage us to learn something:

- On the one hand there are **extrinsic** reasons for learning – where you choose to learn something not for the pleasure of the learning itself, but as a step towards something else. An example might be to work towards a qualification which will enable you to seek a promotion or career change.

- These contrast with more **intrinsic** reasons for learning – where you want to learn something because you believe you will find the learning experience positive in itself. Intrinsic reasons for learning are more likely to be driven by your own search for personal growth, fulfilment or satisfaction. An example might be seeking to develop team leadership skills because you enjoy the experience of working in teams.

These ideas echo those of Herzberg in 1968 who asked 28,000 workers in Pittsburgh what they found satisfying and dissatisfying about their jobs. Herzberg found that people who were happy with their work were satisfied by factors intrinsic to the job such as achievements, recognition, opportunities for advancement, responsibility, growth and the nature of the work itself. On the other hand, people who were less happy with their work tended to be dissatisfied by factors extrinsic to the job such as company policy and administration, supervision, salary and working conditions. Herzberg argues that it is the intrinsic factors that lead people to want to work well.

It seems likely that, in a similar way, if you seek to learn something because you find it intrinsically interesting and valuable then you are more likely to enjoy the experience, and more likely to persevere when the going gets tough. If you are learning something for extrinsic reasons, then you are less likely to enjoy it, and may find it harder to remain committed.

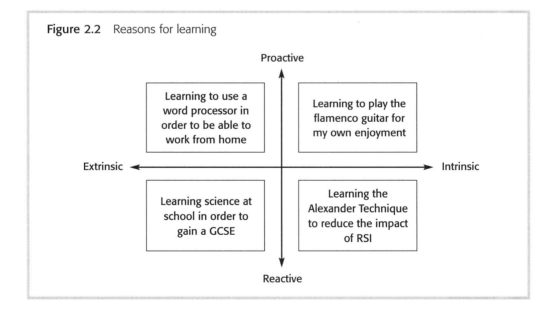

Figure 2.2   Reasons for learning

It is possible to analyse all your learning experiences according to whether you undertook them for intrinsic/extrinsic and proactive/reactive reasons, using a grid as shown in Figure 2.2. This figure uses some of my own examples.

Different people may of course put their reasons in different places – some may well find learning science or computer programs intrinsically interesting. Analysing your grid can help you to make your learning more effective:

- If you are learning for proactive and intrinsic reasons then the learning is more likely to be enjoyable and effective.

- If some of your reasons for learning are reactive, you will need to take other steps to take charge of the learning. Chapter 10 may help with this.

- If some of your reasons for learning are extrinsic, you will need to take other steps both to keep going, and to remind yourself of why you are doing it and what the longer term benefits may be. In particular, it can help to set regular goals and build in rewards at regular intervals. We look at this now.

The importance of setting goals

Setting goals is a means of choosing what, where, and how to learn in order to:

- Make sure you create regular planned opportunities for learning.

- Turn your reasons for learning into something tangible that you can use to guide and monitor your learning.

Setting goals is a process of clarifying:

- Why you want to learn – your reasons.

- What you want to achieve through your learning.

- When you want to learn.

- Where you will find the opportunities to learn – in formal education or training, through learning in practice, or a combination of the two.

- How you prefer to learn, taking account of your learning lifeline, and your successful and enjoyable learning experiences.

- Who will help you to learn.

You can subdivide your goals into more specific or 'smarter' objectives.

Smarter objectives

- *Specific* – focus on one topic and use clear, simple language.

- *Measurable* – set defined targets against which to assess your performance.

- *Attainable* – you can reasonably expect to achieve them.

- *Relevant* – they should be important enough.

- *Timebound* – you should set a realistic time limit.

And

- *Enjoyable* – provide enough satisfaction to make the hard work worthwhile.

- *Rewarding* – offer enough challenge to provide fulfilment and personal.

Breaking down the barricades

While your reasons provide the driving forces for your learning, they alone will not ensure that your learning is effective. At the same time you may encounter a number of barriers that could reduce your chances of achieving your goals (see Figure 2.3).

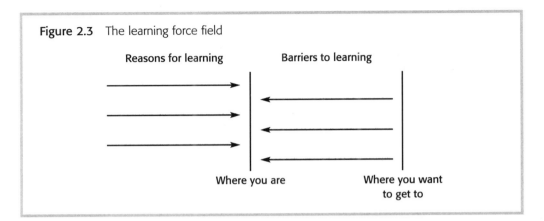

Figure 2.3   The learning force field

Reasons for learning   Barriers to learning

Where you are   Where you want
                                     to get to

It is therefore important to be able to recognise and overcome barriers to learning, which may be personal, practical, organisational or social (see Figure 2.4).

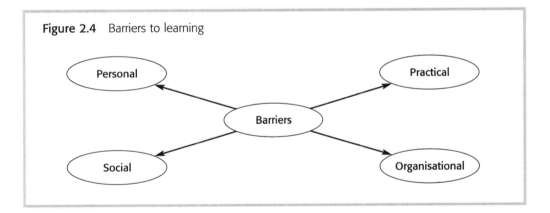

Figure 2.4   Barriers to learning

Personal   Practical

Barriers

Social   Organisational

Personal barriers

Personal barriers to learning may include:

▪ *Negative experiences of learning* – many people have bad memories of school which may influence their perceptions of what learning involves. For example, learning may be associated with failure and this can lead to a lack of self-confidence and self-esteem: as Alan

Rogers comments, in *Teaching Adults*, 'anxiety is a characteristic of most adult learners'.

A negative attitude towards learning – when Naomi Sargent carried out a survey of adult learning, published as *The Learning Divide*, 41 per cent of people claimed they were not interested or didn't want to learn.

Anxiety about the results of learning – what effects may it have on the rest of your life? Might it be safer to remain ignorant?

Lack of learning skills – effective learning depends on using the range of learning skills discussed in this book – see for example, Chapter 5.

Problems in maintaining commitment and keeping going – see for example, Chapter 9.

Practical barriers

Practical barriers to learning may include:

Lack of money and the cost of formal learning programmes.

Lack of time.

Lack of facilities: for example, access to the Internet.

Lack of space: for example, somewhere to read quietly.

Organisational barriers

Most people face at least some personal and practical barriers to learning. But in addition, the organisation may provide further barriers to overcome as well. These **organisational** barriers may include:

The value given to learning – too many organisations still fail to make learning a priority. Development may be seen as a 'luxury' and budgets for learning may be the first to be cut. If learning is seen as a low priority, then attitudes towards learning are likely to be negative as well.

▩ *The way the organisation is structured* – if an organisation is structured along rigid hierarchical lines there may be limited scope for people to learn from each other. Rosabeth Moss Kanter describes what she calls 'segmentalism', where people rarely share ideas and information across departmental divides.

▩ *The way work is carried out* – some ways of working are more likely to encourage learning than others. For example, regular opportunities for delegation and teamwork provide scope for learning; failing to create such opportunities significantly reduces the scope for learning and development.

▩ *The level of support available* – to learn effectively within an organisation, people need access to coaching, mentoring and training. Again, if this support does not exist, people are less likely to learn.

Social barriers

Behind the personal, practical and organisational barriers there may be some broader **social and cultural** barriers. For example, the results of the *1996 General Household Survey* show that, while up to 66 per cent of professional people hold degrees, only between 1 and 2 per cent of manual workers do. Naomi Sargent found that this trend continues into adulthood. While her survey showed that over half of middle class people were current or recent learners, this was true for just a quarter of semi-skilled and unskilled workers. Writing in 1931 Richard Tawney argued that 'the hereditary curse upon English education is its organisation along class lines' and these statistics from the mid 1990s suggest that, while things may have changed, they still have a long way to go.

Reasons for these inequalities are complex and include the relative wealth and power of different groups. However, another important factor is social and cultural attitudes: Richard Hoggart, in his in-depth study of working class culture, *The Uses of Literacy*, describes the then ambiguous attitudes towards education in working class people of Leeds. It seems likely that learning is valued more highly in some parts of society than others. These traditions and attitudes may influence the kind of support that people receive for learning from their family and friends.

Identifying and overcoming barriers to learning

Any barriers to learning won't just go away. It is important to clarify which barriers you face, and to take steps to tackle them. One way of doing this is to use a technique called forcefield analysis.

Forcefield analysis was first described by Kurt Lewin in his book *Field Theory in Social Science*. In this book, Lewin discusses his views about how change happens in organisations, and suggests that organisations can use forcefield analysis to explore any change process. The technique is therefore widely used by change strategists, and you may be able to use it in other contexts – but it is equally applicable to looking at barriers to learning (see Figure 2.5).

Any barriers to learning won't just go away. It is important to clarify which barriers you face, and to take steps to tackle them.

The principle of forcefield analysis is that in any context there are forces for and against change, and that we can influence these to increase our chances of success.

One of the major barriers to learning is our own – and other people's – views about how much we can learn. The next chapter goes on to look more closely at how you learn and how you can make the most of your strengths as a learner.

Figure 2.5   Using forcefield analysis to tackle barriers to learning

1 Create a chart like the one below which shows both where you are now and where you hope to be once you have achieved your learning goals.

2 On the left-hand side, make a list of all the forces in favour of your learning. These may include your reasons for learning, support from colleagues, friends and family, and so forth. You may like to show the relative strength of the forces by making some arrows thicker than others.

3 On the right-hand side, list all the barriers to learning. You will now have a picture of the forces both supporting and opposing you.

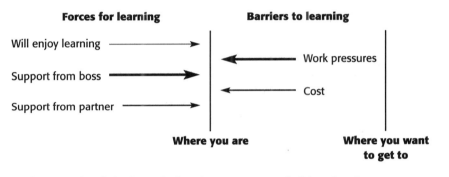

4 Then consider all the forces for learning. How can you build on these?

5 Then consider the barriers to learning. How might you reduce these?

6 Finally, decide on the main actions you will take.

3 Learning with style

You are a visualist. This means that you learn best by . . .

Don't we all love these kinds of inventories? We answer a few pages of questions about ourselves and – hey presto – our real character is identified. We feel we know more about ourselves or some aspect of our life – be it learning or love. It's quick, easy and doesn't involve any effort.

But, it's not as simple as that.

Too many people have taken the wrong message from these questionnaires. They assume that the picture they present of an individual's approach to learning is fixed and set in concrete. This is a shame; there is, in fact, a great deal of research into the question of learning style and it is worth reviewing this research. It can help you to gain a better understanding of how you learn and what has shaped this. And the key message is one of flexibility. You can use your self-awareness of your present approach to become a truly effective learner, equipped with a well-balanced repertoire of styles.

This chapter introduces the key research that has been carried out into learning style and looks at how you can use this to develop and improve your own approach to learning. The chapter explores:

■ Learning style: more than a buzzword? – is learning style a personality trait? Is one style better than another?

- Stripping off the labels: broadening your learning style – the risks of labelling.

- The impact of self-esteem – how self-esteem affects learning style.

- What are your attitudes and approach to learning?

Learning style: more than a buzzword?

There are many terms used to describe the different ways in which individuals approach their learning. These include learning style, learning approach, learning orientation, learning strategy and learning skills. This variety has resulted in some difficulties in arriving at clear definitions. For example:

- One researcher suggests that an individual's tendency to adopt a particular strategy for learning can be referred to as a **learning style**.

- Another defines an **approach to learning** as the learning processes that emerge from learners' perceptions of the learning task as influenced by their personal characteristics. . .

- . . . and goes on to say that the approach is represented in a **learning strategy** which is a self-conscious and planned approach to learning.

In this chapter we begin by explaining two contrasting approaches to learning, before going on to look at some other ideas about learning styles.

Deep and surface learning

A central theme in research on learning styles is the notion of two main approaches to learning: often known as 'deep' and 'surface' learning. A deep approach is one where the learner looks for understanding and meaning; a surface approach is where the learner memorises and reproduces what they learn.

The idea of the importance of 'deep' learning is not new, In 1916, Dewey wrote:

The depth to which a sense of the problem sinks determines the quality of the thinking which follows and any habit of teaching which encourages the pupil to glide over the thin ice of genuine problems reverses the true method of mind training.

Democracy and Education (Dewey, 1916)

Noel Entwhistle, now Director of Education at Newcastle University, is the British researcher who has done most work on learning styles. Entwhistle's team used the combination of a large-scale survey followed by in-depth interviews – an early piece of research involved 767 first year students from nine departments in three British universities.

Entwhistle set out to compare 'deep' approaches, which involve asking questions and seeking understanding, with 'surface' approaches which focus on memorisation and utilisation. Following his research, Entwhistle has described how these approaches involve a range of styles and attitudes.

A **deep approach** is characterised by:

- *Comprehension learning* – where the learner looks for understanding and meaning, and uses questions and analogies to help gain this understanding.

- *Intrinsic motivation* – where the learner is interested in learning for its own sake (we discussed intrinsic reasons for learning in Chapter 2).

- *Openness* – where the learner is open to new ideas, and sees their learning as an opportunity to question values (as in the case with *The Questioning Learner* and *The Creative Learner*).

- *Internality* – the learner is driven by the desire to structure their own learning.

A **surface approach** is characterised by:

- *Operation learning* – the learner adopts a step-by-step, logical approach with an emphasis on finding and memorising facts.

▓ *Extrinsic motivation* – the learner sees learning simply as a way of gaining qualifications or promotion (again mentioned in Chapter 2).

▓ *Fear of failure* – the learner tends to be anxious about learning and concerned that they may not do well.

▓ *Syllabus bound* – the learner relies on clear instructions, structure and a tightly defined syllabus.

Entwhistle also describes what he calls a 'strategic approach' where learners are motivated principally by achievement, adopting a competitive approach with organised study methods and regular habits. These learners are often cynical and disenchanted with learning and place greater emphasis on the social opportunities which it offers.

Table 3.1 summarises the main features of 'surface' and 'deep' learning approaches.

Table 3.1   'Surface' and 'deep' learning approaches

	Surface	Deep
Motivation	Reactive, extrinsic	Proactive, intrinsic
Orientation	Reproducing facts	Understanding meaning
Attitude	Fear of failure	Open to new ideas
Structure	Externally imposed	Internally driven

Other terms for deep and surface learning

Gordon Pask (1988) claims that research supports the reality of distinct and idiosyncratic learning styles and proposes two 'dominant' styles: *holist*, concerned with deep or comprehension learning and *serialist*, concerned with surface or operation learning. Other ways in which these two approaches have been described include 'global and analytic' and 'reinterpretation and atomistic'.

So how can you use these ideas to improve your own learning?

A deep approach pays off . . .

If you are looking for success in your learning, the research consistently underlines that you are more likely to succeed if you use a deep approach.

For example, Entwhistle found that students who tried to memorise a text did less well than those who tried to understand it. And in Sweden two researchers, Marton and Saljo, looked at how students approached understanding a text. They found that what was important was whether students focused on the text itself or on the author's intention and conclusions to be drawn.

. . . but it also pays to be versatile . . .

You are also most likely to succeed if you adapt your learning to the task – by using a 'versatile' style of learning. There is considerable support for the view that higher level learning requires a style which combines both deep and surface learning.

. . . and adventurous

And successful learners are also curious and indeed adventurous. In the 1950s, Roy Heath carried out interviews with students early on in their courses at Princeton University. He identified three 'personality types':

- **Non-committers** have a marked tendency to avoid involvements and are passive in a conflict. Heath suggests that the reason these people choose to be neutral is because they maintain a myth about high potential – they could do a lot of things if they really went all-out. The risk, however, is that if the myth was put to the test they could discover that it has no basis in fact.

- **Hustlers** thrive on purposeful activity, are competitive and prefer logical, factual materials to subjective judgement. Hustlers are often aggressive and insensitive to the feelings of others, which is unfortunate because this type really needs to be thought of favourably and has an inordinate need for achievement and recognition. In reality they are at war with themselves and need to attain success to offset the 'weaknesses' which they believe lie within.

▓ **Plungers** are at the mercy of their feelings, have highs and lows and tend to overreact. They work in spurts and their thoughts, which are highly individualistic – even surreal – zip from one idea to another without apparent connection. They have difficulties with communication and with making their ideas comprehensible to others.

We disagree with Heath's inference that these are personality types – for us they are behaviours that different people may show in different learning contexts. What is, however, interesting in Heath's research is what he calls an 'ideal of development' rather than a personality type – the **reasonable adventurer** whom Heath believed showed the characteristics which were most likely to result in successful learning.

The reasonable adventurer starts learning during an intensive, exciting period with lots of curiosity, before narrowing in on a point of specific interest. This is followed by detachment – reflecting on the meaning of what he discovered during the involved stage.

The reasonable adventurer is characterised by the following attributes:

▓ intellectuality

▓ close friendships

▓ independence in value judgements

▓ tolerance of ambiguity

▓ breadth of interest

▓ sense of humour.

When Heath looked at degree results, he found that the reasonable adventurers did best, the non-committers and plungers both did relatively well while the hustlers did worst of all.

There are clear connections here with other themes in this chapter and in the book – not only do reasonable adventurers adopt a deep approach to learning, they also follow the learning cycle introduced in

Chapter 6, reflect on what they experience and embody many of the characteristics of creativity described in Chapter 7.

Stripping off the labels – broadening your learning style

Most of the literature on learning style relates to academic learning; there is less covering work-related learning or professional development. However, as someone involved in management or professional development you may already be familiar with the Learning Styles Inventory, developed by Peter Honey and Alan Mumford. This inventory has gained a high level of acceptance and is widely used in human resource development.

Honey and Mumford are occupational psychologists who noticed a pattern emerging from the results of the psychometric tests which they conducted for large employers. They identified four styles:

- **Activist** – who thrives on learning through challenges and new experiences.

- **Reflector** – who tends to be cautious, standing back and observing experiences from different perspectives.

- **Theorist** – who adapts and integrates observations into logically sound theories.

- **Pragmatist** – who likes to try out new ideas, theories and techniques to see if they work in practice.

They argue that we all develop our own characteristic profile across these four styles. On hearing Peter Honey talk on a number of occasions about the use and interpretation of the inventory, he has stressed a number of points:

- That a person's learning style is not 'fixed' and that it is capable of change, and indeed frequently does change in response to a range of external influences.

■ That the information about themselves which a person gains from the results should not be used to avoid particular types of learning, rather it should provide a basis for developing a learning approach which results in a more balanced profile.

The risks of labelling

However, some people have tended to use the inventory as a typology – dividing people into discrete categories. In recent research which she carried out with open learners studying for professional qualifications, Anna came across a number of unprompted remarks based on this inventory. For example:

I've come out as a reflector, so obviously I don't like to do activities where you have to jump up and do things.

I get bored with all the theory but that's probably because I'm a pragmatist.

These learners have pinned labels on themselves. They believe that once they have identified their learning style, this is a fixed personality trait which cannot be changed. They must therefore learn to keep within their limitations, seeking out experiences which require their preferred style and avoiding those which invite a different approach.

This view is reinforced by trainers and educators who talk about the importance of planning learning programmes so that they 'cater for different learning styles' and only strengthens the idea that people are only really capable of learning in one particular way. Again, this labels and pigeonholes people – and it is precisely the opposite of the message that Honey and Mumford intended!

Other researchers have voiced concern about the idea of encouraging learners to adopt a particular learning style. For instance, by drawing attention to the danger of increasing the competences of an individual in a limited set of styles at the expense of others and warning us against the idea that one approach is 'best'.

There are indeed several reasons why you should avoid labelling yourself with a particular style:

- *The importance of versatility* – there appear to be clear advantages to adopting a range of styles and approaches in different contexts, rather than sticking with a single style and approach.

- *A lack of consensus* – there are concerns about the reliability of typologies of learning styles.

- Your own *self-knowledge* is at least as important as your preferences for particular styles.

The importance of versatility

If you are to be a versatile learner, adopting a range of styles and combining different approaches as appropriate, then it is absolutely vital to avoid adopting one style of learning at the expense of others.

> *There are indeed several reasons why you should avoid labelling yourself with a particular style.*

   We recommend that if you have a strong disposition towards one particular style you should actively seek out opportunities to apply and develop other approaches. Try to use the insights you get from inventories such as Honey and Mumford's as the starting point for improving and *expanding* your repertoire of learning styles rather than *narrowing* it.

Demonstrating versatility

The capacity of successful learners to be versatile was demonstrated in 1982 by Saljo, the Swedish researcher, who found that using different types of questions in a test can affect the approach to learning. In Saljo's experiment two groups of students were given three separate passages of prose and asked a series of questions after each one. One group was given questions designed to encourage a deep approach, while the other group was asked specific, factual questions intended to induce a surface approach.

After the third passage and questions, both groups were given a further set of mixed questions. Saljo found that students in the 'surface' group who had initially adopted a deep approach had shifted to a surface approach, suggesting that they were able to adapt their approach according to what was required. However, most of the students who had originally used a surface approach found it harder to move to a deep approach.

This research shows how versatile and successful learners are able to adapt their approach to meet the requirements and demands of different learning contexts.

A lack of consensus

Despite the volume of research, there is still no general agreement over how individual learning styles can be identified and classified. Indeed, there is no overall acceptance of the concept of individual learning styles. For example, Robert Gagné sees a problem in relating mental processes to individual differences, and argues that there is no general agreement on methods to measure learning variables.

Claire Weinstein, who has written widely on learning style both in Britain and the US, claims that there is no one scheme that is generally accepted as a way of classifying learning strategies. Writing in 1992 with Crozier she argued that measures to assess the use of particular learning strategies are often unreliable, and give little information. Reasons to be wary include:

- The measures often reflect the importance attached to different skills by different authors.

- The emphasis placed on behaviours, thoughts and activities that correlate with successful study may not be the direct cause of success or achievement.

- Studies which identify correlations between learning styles and achievement cannot show direct causal relationships.

- The need to question whether it is legitimate to infer learning styles from students' self-descriptions of their study behaviour – a method commonly used in such research.

There is also a significant body of thought which disputes claims that individuals have their own inherent learning style at all, or that this is the primary influence on attitudes and success in learning. Other factors have an equally important influence on the approach you might take when studying. For example:

▢ Your reasons for learning (see Chapter 2).

▢ The context within which you learn (see Chapter 4).

▢ Barriers to learning, such as external distractions.

A whole range of factors such as these need to be taken into account when looking at ways to improve learning and it is therefore:

... useless to seek generalisable principles for improving student learning in the characteristics of students, teaching, subject matter, assessment and learning tasks taken singly.

'Context and strategy: situational influences on learning' (Ramsden, 1988)

All this adds up to a major note of caution – while you may be able draw some useful lessons from the research into learning styles, you need to look at it critically.

Learner know thyself

Perhaps the most important aspect of learning style is the insights which the individual adult learner gains into him- or herself as a learner. We agree with Smith who in *Learning how to Learn* suggests that precision in determining learning style should not be the desired outcome of using inventories, rather that they can help people to make choices about how, when and where to learn.

We can all benefit from a greater awareness of our own learning style in order to maximise our strengths and identify our need for development.

We can all benefit from a greater awareness of our own learning style in order to maximise our strengths and identify our need for development. Reissman claims that 'typically, people do not know their own style nearly well enough' and that it is this lack of awareness which leads people to adopt inappropriate methods.

Perhaps trainers, developers and teachers have paid too little attention to these aspects of learning and should help learners to develop greater awareness of learning processes and styles.

Developing self-knowledge

One technique that we have used to help develop self-knowledge in a range of contexts is an activity which asks people to reflect on positive and negative learning experiences.

The activity involves selecting two learning experiences:

- one enjoyable and successful
- one that was not enjoyable and successful.

You can then explore the factors that helped to make each experience successful or otherwise – for example, your reasons for learning, how you learned, where you learned and who helped you. Reflecting on your learning like this can help you to identify aspects of learning that you are good at. It can also help you to plan ways of making your learning more effective.

The impact of self-esteem

Good self-esteem is crucial to successful learning in several ways. Your self-esteem is likely to have an influence on your approach to and styles of learning. It is also important to recognise that self-esteem in learning is different from self-esteem more generally – people who are confident in other aspects of their lives may have low self-esteem when it comes to learning.

The importance of self-esteem

Self-esteem is the personal judgement which a person makes of him- or herself in terms of significance, capability and worthiness. It involves self-evaluation in which an individual compares him- or herself with others. It is dependent upon senses of self-love, self-acceptance and competence. Two definitions are given below – both are clear and accurate:

... a personal judgement of worthiness that is expressed in the attitudes the individual holds towards himself.

The Antecedents of Self Esteem (Coopersmith, 1967)

... an umbrella term under which self image, ideal self and self esteem develop.

Enhancing Self Esteem in the Classroom (Lawrence, 1988)

Adults' images of themselves as learners are powerfully affected by their early school experiences and whether they felt these to be positive or negative – the two main antecedents to a person's self-esteem are early family experience and school. Our own research suggests that people with positive early experiences of learning had greater belief in themselves as learners. Conversely, people who had had poor initial experiences of learning – even those who had later been successful – often needed more reassurance and guidance.

This view is supported by those who argue that quality in early learning can encourage positive, lasting learning patterns and research which has found that self-esteem was significantly related to a child's self-attributions about success or failure and academic achievement.

Many adult learners who have returned to study choose to learn because they want a 'second chance' at education; indeed, the National Extension College was established with this precise aim and the Open University is well known for providing higher education opportunities to adults who missed out first time round. In adult learning there is often less of the competitive element which can be present in conventional learning, and which can be daunting to a learner who lacks confidence. In a pilot study with 30 adult students Anna found 'becoming more confident' as an important reason for learning for nearly half the respondents.

The links between self-esteem and learning style

There is evidence of correlation between learning style and self-esteem. McCarthy and Schmeck (1988) laim that there is a significant relationship between self-esteem and choice of learning strategies, arguing that the integration of deep and surface approaches requires a reserve of unconditional self-esteem. Further research found that subjects who preferred to elaborate on information when studying reported higher self-esteem, which suggests that deep and elaborative strategies are self-assertive in nature, while shallow strategies are more passive and dependent. A study of gifted children found that subjects with high self-esteem used more sophisticated learning strategies. There is also evidence of a positive correlation between self-esteem and achievement.

However, it has been difficult to find an adequate tool to measure self-esteem, and many believe that feelings of self-worth are linked to particular situations rather than being a general or personal trait. So you might have quite high self-esteem in some areas of your life – but still label yourself as a 'failure' in terms of formal learning.

Suppressing the power of learning

John Holt's book *How Children Fail* is essentially a learning diary in which he reflected on episodes in his daily life as a teacher in a New York junior school. His main theme is the relationship between self-esteem and the strategies children adopt to get by in school.

Holt was puzzled by the way in which young children joined the school with open and enthusiastic attitudes to learning but quickly came to adopt strategies more concerned with minimising failure than with maximising their potential.

'But there is an important sense in which almost all children fail: except for a handful, who may or may not be good students, they fail to develop more than a tiny part of the tremendous capacity for learning, understanding, and creating with which they were born and of which they made full use during the first two or three years of their lives.'

He came to the conclusion that the way the school was organised, particularly in terms of rewards and punishments, gave children the message that they should keep their heads down and avoid situations where they might be shown to be 'wrong' or 'silly'. When asked a question, many of his students would hedge their bets:

'He cannot stand uncertainty or failure. To him, an unanswered question is not a challenge or an opportunity, but a threat. If he can't find the answer quickly, it must be given to him, and quickly; and he must have answers for everything.'

For Holt, the result of these 'fail safe' strategies is that schooling may come to suppress our natural power of learning, so that for the rest of our lives opportunities to learn are missed or even shunned.

Labelling and self-esteem

Labelling can also have an impact on self-esteem. People who are labelled as poor learners at school can find it very hard to shake off this label in adult life, while those who are labelled as good learners are more likely to be confident in later learning.

As with learning styles, it is crucial to challenge labels. As we have argued throughout this book, learning is something natural and human, something we are all good at. If you need any convincing that labels must be ignored, just think of the music teacher who labelled John Lennon as being no good at music – or the sports master who labelled Alan Shearer as being no good at football!

How do you learn?

If the most important aspect of learning styles and approaches is your own self-knowledge, then it makes sense to explore your own attitudes and approach to learning in greater detail. There are several ways of doing this:

- You may like to try out one of the learning style questionnaires. We present one, from our own research, on pages 60–63.

- You will find out more about how you learn by reflecting on your own learning. Chapter 6 suggests ways of doing this.

- You will be able to explore your scope for learning both independently and collaboratively in Chapters 8 and 9.

■   You will be able to refine your critical questioning technique in Chapter 8.

Learning questionnaires: here's one I made earlier

Anna used the questionnaire that follows in her own research into how people learn. She designed the questionnaire to identify two aspects of learning – participants' attitudes to learning and the approaches and strategies they use – and in the process explored six key concepts, as follows:

For **attitudes to learning**, the concepts are:

■   self-esteem in learning

■   confidence about your ability to learn

■   previous experience of learning as positive or negative.

For **approach to learning**, the concepts are:

■   need for social interaction

■   learning style: reflection and understanding as opposed to application

■   need for guidance and support.

■ ## Questionnaire Part 1: Your attitudes to learning

Your self-esteem in learning

I consider myself to be better at learning than most people	Strongly agree	Agree	Disagree	Strongly disagree
It takes me longer than others to grasp concepts	Strongly agree	Agree	Disagree	Strongly disagree
On the whole I consider myself to be good at learning	Strongly agree	Agree	Disagree	Strongly disagree

▶

Other people are usually better at learning than me	Strongly agree	Agree	Disagree	Strongly disagree
I generally find it easy to pick up new ideas	Strongly agree	Agree	Disagree	Strongly disagree
Overall I see myself as a bit of a failure as a learner	Strongly agree	Agree	Disagree	Strongly disagree

Your confidence about your ability to learn

I have a lot of confidence in myself as a learner	Strongly agree	Agree	Disagree	Strongly disagree
I tend to worry about whether I'm working to the right standard	Strongly agree	Agree	Disagree	Strongly disagree
I consider myself to be more confident about learning than most people	Strongly agree	Agree	Disagree	Strongly disagree
I am often apprehensive about a new learning experience	Strongly agree	Agree	Disagree	Strongly disagree
I'm always sure that I will be able to achieve the requirements of a course	Strongly agree	Agree	Disagree	Strongly disagree
I think I am more nervous about learning than most people	Strongly agree	Agree	Disagree	Strongly disagree

Your previous experience of learning

Throughout my life I have always enjoyed learning	Strongly agree	Agree	Disagree	Strongly disagree
I have had a fair number of negative learning experiences	Strongly agree	Agree	Disagree	Strongly disagree
I have always been a successful learner in the past	Strongly agree	Agree	Disagree	Strongly disagree
I have tended to find learning and studying a painful experience	Strongly agree	Agree	Disagree	Strongly disagree
On the whole my experience of learning has been positive	Strongly agree	Agree	Disagree	Strongly disagree
I feel I have been a failure as a learner in the past	Strongly agree	Agree	Disagree	Strongly disagree

Questionnaire Part 2: Your approach to learning

Your need for social interaction

Talking to other learners is an essential part of learning for me	Strongly agree	Agree	Disagree	Strongly disagree
I learn best when I work alone	Strongly agree	Agree	Disagree	Strongly disagree
I usually make a contribution to group discussions	Strongly agree	Agree	Disagree	Strongly disagree
I find group discussions are often unproductive	Strongly agree	Agree	Disagree	Strongly disagree
I learn best in a group situation	Strongly agree	Agree	Disagree	Strongly disagree
I rarely say anything in a group session	Strongly agree	Agree	Disagree	Strongly disagree

Your learning style

I have to try out ideas and techniques to fully understand them	Strongly agree	Agree	Disagree	Strongly disagree
I learn things best by reading and thinking about them	Strongly agree	Agree	Disagree	Strongly disagree
I find it easier to grasp an idea when I have to put it into practice	Strongly agree	Agree	Disagree	Strongly disagree
I need time to reflect before I take on new ideas	Strongly agree	Agree	Disagree	Strongly disagree
One of the ways I learn best is by trial and error	Strongly agree	Agree	Disagree	Strongly disagree
I like to feel I have fully mastered a concept or technique before I put it into practice	Strongly agree	Agree	Disagree	Strongly disagree

Your need for guidance and support

I prefer to have step-by-step instructions when I am learning	Strongly agree	Agree	Disagree	Strongly disagree

I only want help and guidance when I have a particular problem	Strongly agree	Agree	Disagree	Strongly disagree
I need a lot of reassurance that I am working along the right lines	Strongly agree	Agree	Disagree	Strongly disagree
I rarely get as much guidance as I would like when studying	Strongly agree	Agree	Disagree	Strongly disagree
I'm happy to get on with my study without a lot of encouragement/support	Strongly agree	Agree	Disagree	Strongly disagree
I prefer to get on with learning rather than have a lot of help and advice	Strongly agree	Agree	Disagree	Strongly disagree

This questionnaire may have given you some insights into your own learning experiences. You can use these insights to:

- Identify things that have helped you to enjoy learning and to learn successfully. These are things you can build on in your future learning.

- Identify labels or preconceptions that you need to challenge.

- Identify areas that you may be able to work on and improve – possibly with help from other people – see Chapter 8 for more on collaborative learning.

But central to getting rid of labels is the idea of empowerment – one of the three Es introduced in Chapter 1. The next chapter looks at what you can do to become a powerful learner.

Becoming a powerful learner

Libraries gave us power.
Then work came and made us free.

The opening lines of *A Design for Life* by the rock band the Manic Street Preachers highlight an important tradition in democratic thought: the idea that learning is essential to becoming a fully enfranchised member of society. This idea has underpinned many of the educational achievements of this century: both the general widening of access to educational opportunities, and more specific initiatives designed to bring learning to the disenfranchised, such as the founding of Ruskin College, Oxford and the Workers' Educational Association in the UK, or the literacy campaigns in Latin American countries. At the heart of this idea lies the belief that learning, by unlocking access to knowledge, offers the key to challenging the power structures in society and organisations.

The chapter explores:

- Learning: the gateway to power – can learning really lead to empowerment?

- Tasting the forbidden fruit – unlocking access to knowledge.

- Deschooling the organisation – changing your relationship with educators and creating a climate for learning.

▓   Becoming a powerful learner – the chapter concludes by introducing the main skills of the powerful learner. This serves as an introduction to Chapters 5–10 which will explore these skills in greater detail.

Learning: the gateway to power

Powerlessness corrupts. Absolute powerlessness corrupts absolutely.

Rosabeth Moss Kanter

Chapter 1 argued that empowerment is one of the vital three Es of learning, and that learning can help empower us to play a full and active role both within the organisation, and in the wider society.

However, it would be wrong to suggest that all learning leads to empowerment. Karl Marx, in his *Economic and Philosophic Manuscripts of 1844*, argued that processes which lead to the creation of knowledge for some may actually leave other people feeling disempowered. As we write this, there is evidence that some people in the knowledge industries certainly feel disempowered – staff at BT call centres are on strike over their conditions of work, and people in third world countries are earning low wages producing microchips.

So what factors may influence whether learning results in empowerment? Which influences help determine whether knowledge leads, in Marx's terms, to intelligence or idiocy? We begin this chapter by looking a little more closely at what power is, before going on to introduce some important ways in which you can help ensure that learning can be an empowering experience.

What is power?

Power is a complex idea and for this reason there are contrasting views about how people become powerful. We discuss two perspectives here.

The visible perspective

The first perspective – the visible perspective – looks at power at the level of the individual. By observing how people behave within their social relationships – in contexts like meetings, negotiations and organisational changes – it is possible to detect their influence over others. This in turn allows us to infer their power base within the team or the wider organisation.

Max Weber, the sociologist, has been influential in this perspective. Weber identified three types of authority in society:

- *Charisma* – this is an individual's personal authority which results from their personality.

- *Tradition* – this is authority resulting from tradition – for example, the authority of professionals such as doctors.

- *Rational/legal* – this is authority which results from a person's position in the organisation – for example, as a senior manager.

Weber believed that an individual's authority could stem from economic, social or political sources. Many modern writers about organisations have developed Weber's views – Charles Handy, for example, or Andrew Kakabadse. They argue that a person's power may stem from a range of sources – their position in the organisation, their ability to offer rewards to others, their expertise or their ability to use contacts and 'pull strings'. This view of power is pluralistic – while some people will be more powerful than others, many people in an organisation will have access to some sources of power.

This perspective gives us some important insights into the relationship between learning and power: in particular the ideas of 'expert' power – the power that individuals draw from their knowledge or expertise – and 'information' power – where people can decide whether or not to release information.

The structural perspective

The second perspective – the structural perspective – looks at power at the level of the wider society. From this perspective, power is an aspect of the social structure used by the strong to protect their interests. Far from being legitimate authority, power is an instrument of oppression, a means for maintaining the status quo. To an important extent, power is hidden – those with power in the social structure have erected an ideology to legitimate their position, and to blind the powerless to the inequalities they face.

This perspective owes much to the ideas of Marx and, to a certain extent, Freud, both of whom believed that human behaviour could only be explained by radical reflection and analysis of deeper structural influences. It has been developed by the critical theorists such as Jurgen Habermas and Paulo Freire, whom we will meet later in this chapter.

This perspective has given us the idea of learning as empowerment. Freire, for example, sees empowerment as a means of redressing the structural balance of power by enabling people to confront and deal with their powerlessness.

The conditions for empowerment

We have briefly introduced these two perspectives in order to illustrate some important insights into how learning and power are related; in particular:

▪ That certain types of knowledge may provide sources of power within an organisation.

▪ That for learning to lead to empowerment we must pay attention both to what we learn, and how we learn it.

In consequence, three conditions for empowerment underpin our ability to become powerful learners:

▪ **What we learn** – and in particular our understanding of the relationship between knowledge, values and interest.

- **Who can influence our learning** – and in particular the relationships we build with educators and across the wider organisation.

- **How we learn** – and in particular our skills and maturity as learners.

Power and reading in Brazil

The enormous potential of these three conditions for empowerment is revealed by Ivan Illich's account of Paulo Freire's work on literacy projects in Brazil, introduced in Chapter 1. He describes how, when villagers met with Freire's teachers in the evening, they would discuss key words which had important meaning for them and the teachers would write these words on the blackboard.

The combination of *what* the villagers were learning – words and ideas that mattered to them such as access to a well – *who* was working with them in the form of radical educators, and *how* they learnt – their growing skills in literacy and democracy – made a powerful impression on Illich. He describes how, as the words remained on the blackboard after they were spoken:

'The letters continue to unlock reality and make it manageable as a problem. I have frequently witnessed how discussants grow in social awareness and how they are impelled to take political action as fast as they learn to read. They seem to take reality into their hands as they write it down.'

Deschooling Society (Illich, 1971)

These three conditions for empowerment will form the focus of the rest of this chapter – and indeed for much of the rest of the book.

Tasting the forbidden fruit – unlocking access to knowledge

In 1641, England stood on the brink of civil war. The years that followed saw armed conflict between the English parliament and King Charles I, the defeat and execution of the king, and the establishment of a republic. These world-shattering events created a heady atmosphere of new ideas about liberty and democracy and a large number of radical groups such as the levellers, diggers, ranters and quakers sprung up.

For nearly 20 years the country experienced a brief period of remarkable press freedom. In *The World Turned Upside Down*, Christopher Hill describes how the now readily available printing presses, combined with the lifting of censorship, enabled the new radical groups to publish 'a continuous flow of pamphlets on every subject under the sun'.

Both the atmosphere of liberty and the flowering of press freedom were short-lived – Cromwell's tolerance decreased with years in power, and the restoration of Charles II in 1660 saw the end of the English republic and the return of censorship. However, this was not to be the only period when increased access to knowledge and greater freedom went hand in hand.

Two hundred years earlier, towards the end of the fifteenth century, the Renaissance had led to the flowering of new ideas right across Europe. In what is now Germany, the radical theologians Erasmus and Martin Luther had seized on the invention of the printing press to make available the fruits of the tree of knowledge previously forbidden to all but the select few working in monasteries or universities. The combination of new ideas and a new method for publicising them was to lead to the reformation and the birth of the protestant religion.

And two centuries after the English Civil War, as democracy based on universal suffrage began to emerge towards the end of the nineteenth century, public libraries were established with the express aim of making knowledge more widely available. Hand in hand with the extension of primary education, the libraries helped underline the important link between the growth of democracy and the access to knowledge and ideas. Access to knowledge can be used to maintain the status quo, and learning can be used to challenge it.

The broadening of access to knowledge has continued with the availability of cheap paperback books, more accessible newspapers and, most recently, the Internet. We now have a level of access to knowledge unparalleled in history.

So, does the increased access to knowledge lead in itself to empowerment? Certainly, the old adage that 'knowledge is power' is supported by many examples: for instance, the time spent preparing to be a professional, the way Coca-Cola has jealously guarded the secret mix of its soft drink ingredients, or the way people within organisations may hoard what they know.

But acquiring knowledge is not necessarily empowering. In practice, you need to be both selective and critical about the knowledge you acquire.

You need to be both selective and critical about the knowledge you acquire.

The relationship between knowledge, values and interest

Many people would have us believe that there is such a thing as 'pure' knowledge – knowledge that provides an accurate and objective portrayal of the world, unbiased by the beliefs, values and interests of those who provide it. This view stems from the early scientific method, which saw the physical world as a set of objective phenomena behaving to a set of rules that could be readily observed and described.

In practice, however, all knowledge is coloured by the beliefs, values and interests of those who generate it. In some cases, it is easy to spot the interests that lie behind knowledge – for example, advertising or political propaganda. In these cases you know that you are being persuaded to buy something or to vote in a particular way, and that while some of the information may be useful – for example, the features of a product or the details of a particular policy – you should treat it with care.

However, even knowledge generated by the most rigorous scientific experiments has still been created within a certain view of the world. This view of the world – which the writer Kuhn called a 'paradigm' – is just one of many such views of the world. Other paradigms – such as Christianity or Greek philosophy – existed before it. Others exist now – and still more are likely to exist in the future.

Consider, for example, the different paradigms within healthcare. People working within the paradigms of Western medicine, Chinese medicine or holistic medicine would all approach a particular condition in very different ways. And even within the same hospital it is quite possible that different staff – for example, doctors and nurses – may operate within different paradigms.

Two paradigms for knowledge

To illustrate the concept of paradigms it is interesting to compare two contrasting views of what knowledge is.

Positivism

The first paradigm – sometimes called **positivism** – argues that knowledge exists in an objective sense. Knowledge is a complex pattern of facts and ideas which we can seek to understand. Several of our 'learning gurus' would, to some extent at least, share this paradigm – for example, the behaviourists such as Skinner or cognitive psychologists such as Piaget or indeed Kolb. For thinkers like this, learning involves absorbing or seeking out this knowledge, and the role of the teacher is to structure this knowledge and make it as accessible as possible to learners.

Constructivism

The second paradigm – sometimes called **constructivism** – argues that we all construct our own personal and social knowledge. This means that knowledge is not just something objective – it is imbued with our own meanings and feelings. In an important way, therefore, everyone's knowledge must be different. For constructivists, teaching and learning are also very different – a teacher cannot 'tell' a learner what to learn; their task instead is to help them to find meaning. Some of the learning gurus who might share this paradigm include Kelly and Rogers.

One of the leading writers on the links between knowledge and interest is Jurgen Habermas, a member of the Frankfurt School of philosophy. In his book *Knowledge and Human Interests*, Habermas argues that different types of knowledge reflect different interests:

■ The knowledge generated by scientific enquiry is designed to help us to control the world – what he calls the 'technical' interest. This type of knowledge reflects the positivist paradigm.

▓ This contrasts with the knowledge we need to understand human relationships – what he calls the 'practical' interest. This type of knowledge reflects the constructivist paradigm.

▓ This contrasts again with the knowledge that can help us to understand the nature of power in society – what he calls the 'emancipatory' interest. This type of knowledge reflects the paradigm of critical theory introduced at the start of this chapter. As Paulo Freire puts it:

> Knowledge emerges only through invention and reinvention, through the restless, impatient, continuing, hopeful enquiry [people] pursue in the world, with the world, and with each other.
>
> *Education: The Practice of Freedom* (Freire, 1974)

Habermas' ideas do of course reflect his own paradigm – he would be among the first people to expect you to look at them critically! And this is the most relevant aspect of his theory: for learning to be empowering we need to be able to look critically at what we learn – and above all to ask critically why a particular piece of knowledge has been created, for which purpose, and in whose interest.

Three traditions for providing knowledge

An important aspect of your critical awareness of knowledge is your understanding of how it is provided, and the different traditions for generating knowledge that exist. For example:

▓ Knowledge produced in the academic research tradition – or paradigm – will have been created according to a specific set of rules. The researchers will have been expected to use a rigorous methodology, and to ask other experts to examine their findings – this is called 'peer review'. The researchers will have worked within a preferred paradigm, and you need to be able to identify this. And it may well be written up in a way that is difficult for lay people to understand.

▓ Knowledge produced in the journalistic tradition will have been created according to a different set of rules. The journalist will seek to make their articles clear, easy to read and indeed entertaining. The writing may be less academically rigorous, but will still be expected to be reasonably correct. It is, of course, subject to the laws of libel.

▓ Knowledge produced on the Internet is again different. Though some information on the Internet will come from academic or journalistic sources, much will not. The wide variety of information sources makes the Internet a creative and exciting place. But it raises further questions about how accurate and reliable the material is.

Chapter 8 will take these ideas a stage further, by discussing how you can use questioning to develop your critical thinking skills.

Deschooling the organisation – changing our relationship with educators

It will be apparent from what you have just read about different paradigms for knowledge that there are also radically different views of the role which educators – whether teachers or trainers – should play. There is power in the relationship between learner and educator – and while this relationship can be empowering, it can also be disempowering.

In his book *Pedagogy of the Oppressed* Freire argues that educators can act either as agents of oppression or forces for empowerment. Freire criticises what he calls the 'banking concept of education' where teachers 'deposit' knowledge in the students who 'patiently receive, memorise and repeat' prior to filing it away and 'storing the deposits' for future use. The 'bank clerk educator' fills people with knowledge, to 'make them more passive still and adapt them to the world' and to discourage creative or critical thinking. This approach is dehumanising – it prevents people from reaching their true potential.

He contrasts this with the role of the 'humanist, revolutionary educator' whose efforts 'must coincide with those of the students to engage in critical thinking and the quest for mutual humanisation'. The educator must possess 'a profound trust' in people and their creative power, and seek to become a partner with them, a 'student among students'.

Freire's ideas are echoed by many other writers. The American psychotherapist Carl Rogers, in his book *Freedom to Learn for the 80s*, used the term responsible freedom to describe the climate in which he had found that both children and adults were best able to achieve their potential as learners:

. . . freedom with responsibility, a freedom in which the excitement of significant learning flourishes.

Rogers's view was that the best teachers create an environment in which individuals are encouraged to play an active and significant part in the learning process. They have freedom to experiment and to influence the style and content of their learning.

Ivan Illich applies similarly radical thinking to the wider organisation. He argues that conventional 'schooling', far from reducing educational disadvantage, actually has an 'anti-educational' effect on society. For Illich, school instruction is neither liberating nor educational because it serves as an instrument of social control. Illich argues that we need to 'deschool' society by increasing the educational role and quality of all organisations.

These challenging ideas suggest that learning is most likely to be empowering when there are both empowering relationships and a wider climate of empowerment.

Some empowering relationships

So what kind of learning relationships can be empowering? Here are some examples:

- **Facilitation**. Rogers argues that teachers need to become 'facilitators' who seek to support and enable the learning process rather than to lead or control it. As Rogers put it, the teacher needs to **permit** the student to learn.

    We worked on a research project which looked at the impact of National Vocational Qualifications (NVQs) on learning. In most of the organisations we contacted the role of teachers and trainers has changed or is changing. Above all, they are increasingly being expected to 'tutor' rather than to 'teach' or 'train'. They are likely to spend more time with individuals and small groups than with 'class' groups, and are more extensively involved in individual negotiation and action planning.

The changing role of teachers

The role of nurse tutors at Charles Frears College of Nursing and Midwifery has changed fundamentally. Prior to the introduction of NVQs they acted as teachers, providing taught courses for day-release learners. Now they provide only one day's induction to new learners and the bulk of their time is spent in supporting learners and coach/assessors in the workplace. This new role involves providing pastoral support, briefing learners and helping them draw up an individual action plan, and keeping in regular touch – by phone or visit.

The nurse tutors meet regularly as a team. They have developed an open atmosphere where everyone raises problems and issues and shares ideas.

Learning partnerships. There can be other empowering relationship which do not involve a specialist educator. One example of this is the 'learning partnership' where two people agree to support each other's learning. This can involve the partners working together on the same topic, meeting up to discuss their progress. It could equally involve two people working on different topics.

Two related ideas are:
— coaching, where a team leader plays an important role in helping members of the team to develop their skills and take on new responsibilities
— mentorship, where someone with experience within the organisation agrees to support someone who is relatively new or inexperienced.

Empowering coaches

At Burton Biscuits in Cwmbran people who had been employed at the company for several years were asked to take on a coaching role. This role has proved empowering for the coaches as well as the people they support: a number of workers commented on how their involvement in work-based learning had encouraged them to take on board new responsibilities and had generally increased their confidence. The following comment was made by a shop-floor supervisor who had become a workplace trainer:

'I never did very well at school – that was a long time ago mind. And here I am training others. I really enjoy that, yes, I do feel good about it.'

Learning webs. It is also possible to create wider support networks, where a number of people with shared interests agree to work together. Illich suggests that such learning webs could bring together people who wish to exchange skills or learn together. The growth of the Internet offers an additional impetus to this idea, and increasingly people are using the Internet as a means of exchanging ideas and support.

Many of the examples of group learning described in Chapter 8 – for example, action learning sets – can also be empowering. The example below shows how groups in one organisation helped staff to learn and develop.

Groups as a basis for empowerment

The Learning Disabilities Directorate of Cornwall Healthcare Trust provides healthcare services to people with learning disabilities throughout Cornwall and the Isles of Scilly. Until 1991 most clients lived in hospitals – however now the Trust has a clear objective that 'no one, regardless of the level of their disability, should have a hospital as a permanent address', and clients live in a network of more than 50 houses and bungalows in residential areas. They are supported by specialist staff and, as appropriate, by psychiatrists, psychologists, community nurses, physiotherapists, speech therapists and occupational therapists.

This change of policy called for a major reprofiling of the services they offered, and the staffing needed to provide these services. Many organisations would have adopted a top-down approach to such a major reorganisation. However the Trust opted to put empowerment at the core of its approach:

- Client needs became the focus for the staff reprofiling. This reflects a broader Trust commitment to providing clients with a real independence and experience of citizenship – clients are tenants in their own homes and are able to play an active part in the life of their communities.

- All staff who would be affected by any changes were actively and genuinely involved at every stage of the process in order to build in their expertise and gain their commitment to the new staffing arrangements.

The Trust sought to involve staff and their representatives through a series of focus group meetings which became the heart of the reprofiling process. Christine Bateman, a local services manager who helped to facilitate focus group meetings, explains how this approach to empowerment worked:

'My role was to facilitate groups, ensuring that people were able to understand the process, to develop their own individual skills, to take part in working within a group, and were able to speak and work and set ideas together.'

The process was to prove a rewarding learning experience for those involved. As Chris Millard, a community nurse commented:

'The reprofiling made me think about what I was actually offering people. It helped me manage my time and actually clarify my role.'

And as a result of staff being so fully involved, the outcomes were beneficial not just to the clients and the organisation, but to staff career opportunities. As Gina Brocklehurst, Chief Executive puts it:

'It means that somebody can actually come into the service as a support worker and progress through the service. There are very clearly identified roles at each level and each role is backed with a very strong education and development profile.'

Creating a climate for empowered learning

It is not just individual relationships that can empower learning. It is also possible to create a wider climate within the organisation which provides opportunities for people to continuously learn and reach their full potential. Writers such as Bob Garratt have talked about this as a 'learning organisation'. Garratt, in his book *Creating a Learning Organisation*, comments that if any organisation is to survive and have a chance of growing then 'its rate of learning has to be equal to, or greater than, the rate of change in the external environment'. He argues that it is vital for organisations to develop 'learning systems' that allow people to learn continuously.

However, this concern with empowerment is not restricted to learning. Several influential management writers, such as Tom Peters and Robert Waterman in *In Search of Excellence*, Rosabeth Moss Kanter in *The Change Masters* and Richard Schonberger in *Building a Chain of Customers*, have stressed the importance for organisations of making a commitment to continuous professional development and empowering people to take real responsibility for what they do, as a key factor which distinguishes successful organisations.

In *Japanese Manufacturing Techniques*, Schonberger points out that in the traditional production line people work in a row. Work is 'pushed' towards them – often at high speed along a conveyor belt – and they must push it on to the next person down the line. There's little encouragement for learning, especially as errors and mistakes are generally not spotted until quality inspection – when it's too late to make changes.

In many Japanese firms, by contrast, production lines are U-shaped or parallel. Conveyor belts are less common – instead people walk to get work when they need it. Because they 'pull' work to them like this any errors are spotted at once by the next person along and together they can try to sort it out.

The U-shape creates a natural team and makes it easier for people to move from one job to another and to help each other. Learning takes place constantly – mistakes themselves provide learning opportunities and managers will stop the line so the workforce can sort things out, rather than letting problems through.

Coats Viyella

We visited the Coats Viyella group, a textile firm supplying clothing to Marks & Spencer, with sites spread across the East Midlands and North East of England. The company had made important changes to the working environment – the production line was organised on a team basis in U-shapes or horseshoes. Each team had a number of workstations and staff could move from one to another depending on the style required. There was considerable flexibility and scope for checking during the process. The team became a forum for learning – staff learned from colleagues both during initial training and beyond.

The company had made the most of these arrangements in planning learning opportunities. The company has always been highly committed to training but whereas in the past staff learned one skill, now they learned a range of skills and were able to use a wider range of machines. The result is a more flexible workforce, a quick response to changes and therefore an ability to meet changing customer requirements.

The company had achieved the Investors in People standard. They were using an Employment Practices Audit in a bid to establish a partnership with the workforce. Their team working practices were the subject of a research project with staff from Sheffield and Manchester Universities.

Such differences are noticeable in many other contexts. Think of the difference between an open-plan office and one where the boss's office is hidden away behind a closed door down a long corridor. Or the difference between a lecture hall and a seminar room.

There are many ways in which the organisational climate will influence learning.

There are many ways in which the organisational climate will influence learning. Our research has suggested that the following factors are especially important:

■ **People are valued** – at the heart of a positive learning climate is a clear commitment to people. This is not simply a matter of saying that people are the most important resource – it is about genuine empowerment, and creating a culture within which people are involved, their views are valued, and they are able to make a full contribution.

Learning has priority – the organisation needs to commit resources to learning so that people can take charge of their development. Senior managers must advocate and openly support learning in the organisation and ensure that there is time for learning to take place, and a culture that supports learning.

BhS – creating a culture of support

When we visited UK retail firm BhS we found a commitment to learning at the very top. The Human Resources Director had a vision of changing the business's fortunes through a better trained workforce. Working closely with a supportive Chief Executive he was able to convince the board that staff development was vital to success. Staff development became a Critical Success Factor for line managers, and each time the Human Resources Director visits a site he asks for an update on progress. This translates into everyday practice – as the HR manager told us:

'The culture of support is very dear to us – our experienced associates should automatically want to encourage people with less experience.'

There is an **atmosphere of teamwork and support** – if people are to learn from work, they need a helpful and supportive atmosphere; they need to know that they can ask for help when they need it, and they need to respond positively to requests for help themselves. As one trainee told us:

You can go to anyone for help. Our home manager is very supportive – she'll encourage me to take time off to spend in the library.

People are prepared to admit and **learn from mistakes** – if an organisation punishes every mistake, people will take fewer chances and cover up if things go wrong. If mistakes are accepted and even valued, people will be open about them and prepared to learn from them.

People are encouraged to **try out new approaches** – if people are not punished unduly for mistakes, they are more likely to try out new ways of doing things. In the process they are likely to find better ways of doing them, which will help the organisation to improve. As one trainee told us:

The group work helps you to work with other people, to learn to take responsibility.

- **Questions are welcomed and encouraged** – it is crucial that people feel able to ask why things are done the way they are done, as we shall see in Chapter 8.

- **Everyone learns all the time** – throughout the organisation people are aware that they can learn continually – from their own work, from their colleagues, from customers and suppliers, and so on. Learning is seen as a normal and natural process, not something confined to a training room. Schonberger, for instance, argues that in a healthy, improving business:
  All employees, from the CEO to bottom-scale new-hire, get on the path of continuous learning and don't ever get off.

Auditing your organisation

Use this checklist to audit the learning climate in your organisation. Give your organisation a score for each statement – 5 if this is completely true and 1 if this is completely untrue.

	Score
People are valued	❑
Learning has priority	❑
There is an atmosphere of teamwork and support	❑
People are prepared to admit and learn from mistakes	❑
People are encouraged to try out new approaches	❑
Questions are welcomed and encouraged	❑
Everyone learns all the time	❑

Few organisations are going to score the full 35 points. But what does your organisation's score tell you about your organisation as a place to work?

Six steps to becoming a powerful learner

This chapter has concentrated on some of the broader issues in empowerment – the need for a critical attitude towards what you learn, the need for empowering relationships and a wider climate of empowerment. But what do you, as a learner, need to become a powerful learner?

We believe that a powerful learner is marked out by a number of characteristics:

- They are **capable** – they have the learning skills to plan, manage and monitor their own learning.

- They are able to **reflect** on experience – they can stand back from the events they encounter at work, and make sure that they learn the maximum from them.

- They are **creative** – they are able to look at problems from multiple perspectives, to come up with alternative solutions, to try out new things and to use their intuition.

- They are capable of **questioning** things – as this chapter has stressed, it is crucial to be able to look critically at how things are done, and to ask the question 'Why?'.

- They are **collaborative** – they are able to work with and learn from other people.

- They are capable of working **independently** – while collaboration is a vital aspect of learning, at the same time you need to be able to work and learn independently.

Together, these characteristics make up six steps to becoming a powerful learner. Chapters 5 to 10 will explore each of these steps in turn. To begin with, Chapter 5 looks at how you can become a capable learner.

5 The capable learner

> Success in the marketplace increasingly depends on learning, and yet most people don't know how to learn.
>
> *Strategy, Change and Defensive Routines* (Argyris, 1985)

We are clear that learning is a natural human function; that human beings are incapable of going about their day-to-day activities without learning – indeed you can't avoid learning. Nevertheless you can develop your learning skills and abilities; you can, so to speak, improve on nature!

This chapter is perhaps the one which is most like a conventional 'how to learn' book. It looks at the techniques and methods which people can use to make their learning more efficient, productive and effective. However, most books about learning begin and end with these ideas. We see them as just one step to powerful learning which emphasises your self-awareness, your knowledge of the learning process and your ability to be dynamic and proactive in relation to learning opportunities.

This chapter explores:

▨ Why learn to learn? – looks at our growing awareness of the value and importance of learning skills.

▨ What makes a capable learner? – discusses some of the main issues in understanding learning skills.

■ Developing your toolkit – some of the most important techniques for learning effectively.

■ How can you improve? – planning to increase your learning capability.

Why learn to learn?

There are important reasons for increasing our awareness of learning skills and for improving our mastery of these skills – making the 'tricks of the trade' explicit rather than implicit. Studies in schools, colleges and universities have shown that when students have been taught to use more effective strategies there is a marked improvement in their achievement.

In the past there has been little or no emphasis on developing study and learning skills in much formal education. It has, however, received greater attention in adult education. Wellesley College offered a course as early as 1894 and from its inception in 1964 the National Extension College has responded to their students' need to develop their study skills – producing *How to Study Effectively* in 1972. One reason for the concentration on study skills in adult education has been the fact that many adults have returned to learning and often lack confidence in their ability to learn. Helping them to recognise and develop their learning and study skills is a powerful way of boosting confidence and reducing anxiety. In 'access courses', which are designed to help adults without A levels to enter higher education, study skills are an integral part of the programme.

Behind the closed door

Shelagh attended an access course before starting (and completing) a degree. The course covered topics such as note taking, time management, reading effectively and learning how to remember as well as general writing skills. She says:

'I was amazed because it was 'unlocking the secrets'. These were things that I had thought mysterious or too difficult for me and I suddenly discovered that it was something you could learn.'

You need to know about the skills and techniques of learning; you need to be able to try them out, talk about them, receive guidance and advice about learning, otherwise you may use a limited repertoire of techniques or apply an inappropriate technique for a particular learning task.

> *You need to know about the skills and techniques of learning.*

Learn these words for a test on Monday

As children many of us were given a list of words by our teacher and told to 'learn them'. This would be followed a few days later by a spelling test. It was actually up to us to work out how to master this 'learning'. From her work in adult basic education Anna learned that many people simply did not know *how* to learn individual spellings:

- Some thought that if they looked at them for long enough then the word would go through their eyes and into their brain – not much use if you don't have good visual memory.

- Others thought that if they wrote out the words enough times then they would remember them – not effective for people who don't respond to kinaesthetic approaches.

The result is that by the time most of these people become adults and have failed to learn to spell they believe themselves to be stupid and incapable of learning. What a waste and a tragedy when there are so many techniques for learning individual spellings.

Anna writes:

'In my own case I have a good aural memory so I learned spellings by using my own 'spelling pronunciation' (a technique which nearly everyone uses to spell the word 'Wednesday'). As a child I assumed that everyone learnt this way. Other methods I used included 'word attack' where you analyse a word to identify the difficult bits or break it down into smaller chunks. However my teachers never discussed or suggested any of these techniques to me.'

Learning skill is a critical issue

The ability to learn about learning and become masters of the learning process is the critical issue for the next century.

A Declaration on Learning (Learning Declaration Group, 1998)

Greater attention is being given to learning skills today. There are several reasons for this. One is our increased knowledge of the topic – as a result of research, we know more about learning skills and strategies and why these strategies work.

Another reason is our wider understanding of the nature of intelligence. Psychologists had previously believed that intelligence was fixed, determined mainly by heredity and defined by intelligence test scores. We now question these beliefs. The discussion has moved on to look at the best ways of describing individual differences in learning and the degree to which learning abilities and skills can be developed.

Teachers of all ages of student are increasingly coming to recognise that helping people develop learning skills is a vital part of their role.

And finally, as we realise that learning is an active process in which the learner has to make choices, we become aware that there are alternative ways of approaching learning situations.

How learning skills can overcome barriers

In their book *How to Win as a Part-time Student*, Phil Race and Tom Bourner describe a survey in which adult learners were asked what aspects of returning to learning they had found to be more difficult than they expected. The main problems were identified as finding time to study, coping with other demands such as hobbies, jobs and family commitments, the stress of exams and developing applied study skills such as essay writing.

As we saw in Chapter 2, one of the biggest barriers to effective learning is lack of confidence or anxiety about learning. Not only does this tend to lead to a surface approach (see Chapter 3) – it can also influence the learning and study skills that we use. One study looked at anxious learners who were very nervous about exams. They had help with reducing their anxiety about exams and tests but still did not do any better. Investigation revealed that this was because they were poorly prepared since their anxiety made them study ineffectively; memorising details, reading and re-reading and becoming rigid in their choice of learning strategy.

Skill or strategy?

You will notice that we talk about learning skills and learning strategies. This is because different writers and researchers use different terms. To clarify things:

- **Learning skills** are specific techniques and behaviours which an individual may apply to a task – for example, note taking, memorising.

- **Learning strategy** is the choice to make use of one or more learning skills as appropriate to a task.

Study skills is the term used most often in books and manuals aimed directly at learners and often looks at ways of preparing to study as well as applying the skills themselves.

What makes a capable learner?

There are a great many guides, books and manuals about learning skills. These include the well known 'how to study' type of guide as well as inventories and activities designed to help identify which learning skills an individual does or does not possess. Claire Weinstein and her colleagues at the University of Illinois conducted an extensive survey of study skills inventories in an attempt to arrive at a definitive list of skills. A number of issues arose during this review:

- There was no consistent definition of study skills.

- Most inventories were not empirically validated.

▓ The inventories were only useful as predictors of academic achievement; they could not be used as a diagnostic tool to identify development needs.

▓ The inventories covered a wide range of skills and couldn't reliably measure sub-sets within them, such as note taking.

▓ Results can be easily faked – learners know what answers to choose to give the impression of good study skills.

▓ While research suggests that there are two components to effective study – consistent, regular study and using an active learning style – most inventories deal only with the first aspect.

As a result of this review they arrived at a learning and study skills inventory summarising the key skills (LASSI).

LASSI – the Learning and Study Skills Inventory

According to Weinstein, you are more likely to learn successfully if you adopt the following strategies. These are listed in alphabetical order – not necessarily in terms of importance.

▓ Anxiety – you avoid being worried, tense or nervous.

▓ Attitude – what you learn is important and relevant to you.

▓ Concentration – you pay attention, listen and are not easily distracted.

▓ Information processing –you fit learning with what you already know, comparing translating information into your own words.

▓ Motivation – you are self-disciplined and willing to work hard.

▓ Scheduling – you use time well and are organised and systematic.

▓ Selecting main ideas – you pick out key ideas and critical points.

▓ Self-testing – you review information regularly and prepare for later sessions.

▓ Study aids – you adopt a broad approach and take advantage of aids such as practice exercises, sample problems, examples and diagrams.

▓ Test strategies – you prepare, know the right things and are flexible when necessary.

Learning skills at work

We have said that much of the research and literature on learning skills is concerned with the requirements of academic courses. This is natural because it is learners in this sort of formal learning situation who are most likely to feel the need for study skills and who researchers can most easily identify. However, good learning skills are just as important in non-formal learning situations as we can see in the example below.

Building blocks of learning

Frank is a highly experienced and competent builder. He has extensive knowledge of many of the building trades and undertakes large-scale projects, mainly in the domestic market. He has had no formal training – not even a traditional apprenticeship – and yet he has managed to acquire a wide range of skills and knowledge.

'I learnt by working with other people who were experts, watching what they do and then doing it myself with them supervising and checking. If I need to learn something new I think about what I need to know and who I might ask and then go and talk to them about it – get advice. When I've done something – say laid a floor – someone else might say, 'I would have done it in such and such a way' and then you think, Yes, that would work. So you build up your ideas about ways of doing things.

'When I hit a problem I try to work it out and usually talk to someone else to get their ideas. I also always read any leaflets or instructions that come with a new appliance or part. It's important to know what you can and can't do; for example I don't touch electrics – to be honest that's partly because it doesn't interest me but I've also had a few nasty shocks.'

Although not in a formal learning situation it is clear that Frank uses many of the strategies in the LASSI inventory. What he learns is relevant, he listens carefully, processes new information with what he already knows, is willing to work hard and can pick out key ideas and critical points.

Indeed, the focus in the literature on academic skills has important limitations – it narrows down learning skills to what might more accurately be termed study skills, and ignores many important skills of workplace learning such as reflection and learning practical tasks. For example, learning from observation is often seen as a 'low level' learning skill – however the ability to synthesise and organise key stages and processes from a demonstration can be just as analytical a procedure as extracting significant messages from an academic text.

What is needed is to have a range of tools and techniques at your disposal and to use the right learning tool for the job.

Much of what we learn we do not learn from books or in a formal setting. As we saw in Chapter 2, most learning is acquired through planned or incidental experiences and episodes. What is needed is to have a range of tools and techniques at your disposal and to use the right learning tool for the job.

And merely knowing about study skills is not enough, Weinstein's research – demonstrating that learners could 'fake' their responses to questionnaires to arrive at a high score – underlines that people probably already know they must practise and apply the skills if they are to be any use. Study and learning skills have to progress so that they become good learning 'habits'. We need to internalise them so that they are part of the day-to-day way in which we go about tackling any learning task.

Developing your toolkit

A survey of a range of books on study skills, methods and techniques – the sort with names like 'Succeed in study', 'How to study', Improve your study skills', etc.– reveals that the most common topics on which the authors give advice are:

- organising and planning learning

- reading critically

- making notes

- remembering
- learning style
- essay writing
- preparing for exams/assessment.

The rest of this chapter looks in more detail at some of these crucial study techniques which are consistently seen as important to success. We do not look at:

- Learning style. This was covered in Chapter 3.

- Essay writing. We do not believe that this *is* a learning skill but see it as a subject-specific skill which is integral to particular programmes or areas of study.

- Preparing for exams and assessment – again not really a learning skill as such.

We will begin by looking at organisational skills, before going on to discuss making notes, reading and memorising.

Organising your learning

It is all too easy to start off with good intentions but to let things slip as your day-to-day routine pushes planning learning towards the back burner. Making learning an active priority depends on discipline and routine. As Graham Gibbs has pointed out (Gibbs, 1981) the three key requirements are:

- *Getting organised* – so you know what you have got to do and how you will fit it into your busy life.

- *Getting down to it* – so that when you have time available you get down to business rather than watching TV, making a cup of coffee, reading a newspaper and so on.

▨ *Sticking at it* – so that once you have got started you do not feel 'Oh well, I've done 15 minutes – perhaps I have got time to watch Coronation Street after all.'

▨ Tips for planning and organising

▨ **Make sure you have somewhere to work** – your own space where you feel comfortable and where you are relatively free from interruptions. Some people find it actually helps to go somewhere like the library where there are fewer chances of getting distracted.

▨ **Keep a list of things to do** – and cross things off when, and only when, you have done them. Make sure the list contains small steps so that rather than putting 'Write assignment' you break this down into plan assignment, get books from library, make notes, do rough draft etc. As well as giving you a sense of accomplishment as you complete each stage it also helps with planning and scheduling for what you actually need to do.

▨ **Set targets and deadlines** – make sure these are realistic and achievable and then be tough with yourself in 'negotiating' extensions!

▨ **Use planning aids** – wall-charts and planners and so on; Personal Information Management (PIM) software if you have a PC/Mac or hand-held computer. This can help you to keep track of how things are going and to see the consequences if you change your plans.

▨ **Recognise when you work best** – find the times of day when you concentrate most easily, think most sharply and have the longest attention span.

▨ Concentrating

Being able to concentrate is a vital part of learning. It involves a number of things:

▨ Reducing *interruptions* to a minimum. Interruptions are external – they may come from other people, surrounding noise, telephone calls and so on.

▨ Clearing your own mind of *distractions*. These come from yourself, other things you have to do or would prefer to do.

▨ Focusing your *attention* clearly on what you are learning, knowing why you are learning and what you want to get out of it.

Making notes

There are three main reasons for making notes as part of your learning:

- As a memory aid – you cannot hope to remember everything about a conversation or article.

- Re-ordering or re-organising material – so that it makes sense to you.

- As an aid to concentration – note taking aids concentration because it is an active process.

Short and sweet

It is important to avoid making notes verbatim or in sentences since it has been shown that 90 per cent of the words in standard notes are not necessary. You should develop note-taking techniques which focus on creating a concept overview using *key* or *creative* words and phrases. This technique works because:

- It avoids wasting time recording and re-reading words which will not help you to remember or understand.

- It clearly highlights the words which are key.

- It strengthens the links between key words and thus makes use of the associative power of memory.

You can practise key word and phrase selection by looking at previous notes you have made and underlining or highlighting what you consider to be the key words.

Mind maps

A development of the idea of key words is the technique of mind mapping which was originated by Tony Buzan. He suggests that since the brain works with key concepts in an integrated and interlinked manner then our notes should also be structured in this way. A mind map starts from the centre with a main theme and branches out with associated ideas and points and each map will have its own distinct appearance.

Figure 5.1 shows a mind map of this chapter created by one of our reviewers.

Figure 5.1   Example of a mind map

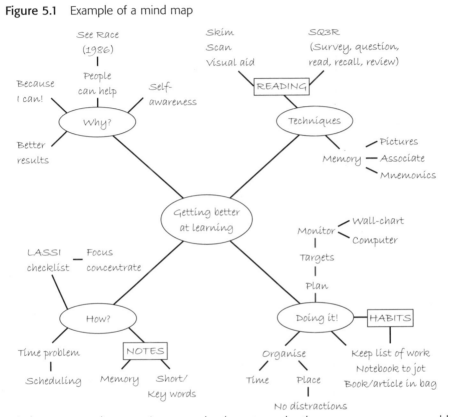

Mind maps can also use pictures and colours to make them even more memorable. Advanced mind-mapping techniques use codes, shapes and arrows to reinforce associations or patterns or to delineate types of information.

The advantages of mind maps are that:

■ The central idea is defined.

■ The relative importance of each idea is made clear – more important ideas are nearer to the centre.

- The links between key concepts are immediately recognisable.

- The structure allows new information to be added without making the notes messy.

Reading effectively

Reading is one of the main ways in which we learn – either as printed text or words on a screen. To read effectively you do not need to approach everything you read in the same way. You would read a memo or letter in a different way from a professional journal or a textbook. The key to effective reading is therefore to choose the right reading technique for the job.

Reading techniques

The three most important reading techniques are as follows:

- **Skim reading** – to skim read you look quickly through the book to get to know your way round it, to check whether it is relevant and to identify parts that you may need to read in detail. To do this you are likely to check the contents, index, headings, introductions and conclusions. You may also check how up-to-date it is by looking at the publication date and author details.

- **Scanning** – you scan when you want to find a key section or word. In the process you ignore all the other parts of the book.

- **Detailed reading** – this is the technique to use when you need to read and understand a passage. See the example below for one technique for reading to understand.

In some cases you may apply just one technique to something you need to read – for example, skimming a journal article to see if it is relevant, or scanning the minutes of a meeting for your own action points. In other cases you might use all three techniques – for example, when you begin reading a book you might skim it quickly to check it is relevant, scan it for the parts you need to read, and then read these closely to understand them.

Survey, Question, Read, Recall, Review

In their book *How to Study Effectively* Richard Freeman and John Meed describe the following five-stage method of approaching a piece of detailed reading. The stages are as follows:

- *Survey*. The first stage is to identify which parts you will read in detail. Like skimming, this involves checking the title, author, date, contents, introduction, index and chapter headings.

- *Question*. You read best if you read with a clear purpose. So the second stage is to ask yourself some key questions about your reading. Why are you reading it? What do you want to find out?

- *Read*. You can then read through the passage – possibly twice, quite quickly. During the initial read you will check that you understand the overall gist. What is the main idea in each paragraph? Which parts are factual and which give the author's ideas? What evidence does the author provide for what he or she is saying? What examples does the author give?

  As you re-read you can move towards an overall judgement on the passage. Are you convinced by the author's ideas? What criticisms might you make? Which ideas could you use yourself? What other ideas might you look for?

- *Recall*. Immediately after reading, try to recall – and possibly note down – the main ideas in the passage.

- *Review*. Finally, look back over the passage and check that your recall was correct. Note down any important points you missed or misinterpreted.

A number of factors can affect your reading and learning. Some of these factors are to do with you – how skilled a reader you are, how interested you are in a topic, how much you already know about it, how keen you are to find out more. Others are concerned with external factors such as the environment or time available. Finally, aspects of the material itself such as the writing style are also an influence. To read effectively you should try to minimise as many negative features as possible – avoid reading if you are too tired, likely to be interrupted, or if you have other pressing concerns on your mind.

Advanced reading techniques

The following advanced reading techniques can be useful:

- **Use a visual aid**. Use a pen or pencil to follow words as you read – rather like children do when they start to read. The faster you move the pencil the faster you read. This may make the reading speed *seem* slow but this is because we tend to think we read faster than we actually do and using a visual aid is in fact a very efficient way of reading.

- **Expand your focus**. Practise taking in more than one line at a time – this is particularly useful for light material or for getting an overview. Use a visual aid, moving down the side of the page, to help you focus.

- **Practise at high speed**. Turn pages as fast as possible and attempt to see as many words per page as possible. This will 'train you up' so that a higher speed of reading becomes routine. After practice you will find yourself reading at twice your previous speed without feeling a difference.

Memory and recall

Many people find that they do not recall very much after hours of learning, even when they have understood everything they have read. This is because memory and understanding do not work in exactly the same way as time progresses. Recall tends to get progressively worse as time goes on unless the mind is given brief rests.

The pattern tends to be that, whilst understanding remains relatively constant, we tend to recall more at the beginning and ends of learning periods and less of the things in the middle of a learning period.

Improve your level of recall

To keep recall at a good level you need to find the point at which recall and understanding work in greatest harmony. This is normally between 20 and 40 minutes of starting to learn. A shorter period does not give you time to get into the rhythm and organisation of the material and a longer period will result in a decline in the amount remembered.

If you arrange for brief breaks in the learning period, at these optimum times, then the level of recall will be kept high. Breaks are also useful as relaxation points and will get rid of muscular tension: particularly important if you are working at a computer screen.

Getting on the right wavelength

Repetition is not always an effective memorising technique. When the BBC was going to change the wavelengths for some radio broadcasts they used saturation coverage to tell listeners about the changes again and again. Afterwards researchers tested a large sample of listeners on their knowledge of the new wavelengths and found that it was virtually non-existent. Yet the frequency of giving the information, combined with the amount of time people listened to the radio, meant that they must have heard it well over 1000 times!

Short and long-term memory

While you may remember what you have just learnt immediately after an episode of learning, you may find that the amount you remember the next day or the next week is significantly less.

This is because recall after a learning period initially rises and then declines quite steeply. Within 24 hours of a one-hour learning period it is normal for at least 80 per cent of detailed information to be forgotten.

The amount you remember can be increased by using review techniques, just before the times that recall is about to drop.

Improve your long-term memory

Using the review technique, the *first review* should take place approximately 10 minutes after a one-hour learning period and last about 10 minutes. This should be a fairly thorough review. If you have made notes you should review and revise these, perhaps even making a new and final copy. This will keep your recall level high for about a day.

The remaining three reviews will each last only 2–4 minutes, during which time you should jot down on a piece of paper everything you remember and then check this against your notes and make any corrections or additions. You might find it helpful to use mind maps for both your notes and your reviews.

The *second review* should take place about 24 hours later – after this recall will probably be maintained for about a week, when a *third review* should take place. Do a *final review* after a month and by this time the knowledge will be stored in your long-term memory.

Mnemonics

Mnemonics are techniques which can help you to remember something more easily and quickly and then to remember it for much longer afterwards. They cash in on the associative and linking power of memory. For example we often remember items which we associate with repetition, rhyming or which are unique or unusual. This can be done by:

- **The use of acronyms** – groups of letters chosen to help you to remember key points or features. A good example is the acronym for Smarter objectives that you met in Chapter 2.

- **Visual imaging** – for example, there are three questions you want to ask in a job interview. You want to know:
  - the organisation's direction and future plans – imagine a signpost
  - their approach to teamwork – add a group of hikers looking at the signpost
  - whether they have a learning centre – the signpost points towards a learning centre.

  You might also use this technique to make sure you remember important achievements that you want to mention.

Increasing your capability

To be a capable learner you need, therefore, to:

- Plan your own learning.

- Organise and manage your own learning.

- Use a range of techniques in order to acquire the information, understanding and skills you need efficiently and effectively.

Increasing your capability in learning is not just a question of adding a few tricks and techniques to what you already do. It involves developing learning habits which become embedded in the way in which you learn and study.

It is important to recognise that this may mean that you need to 'unlearn' certain behaviours and be self-disciplined as you create new ways of working. This is not necessarily an easy task – the following checklist gives some suggestions.

Checklist – becoming a capable learner

- What are my good study habits?
- What new techniques could I make use of?
- What are my poor study habits?
- How can I change these?
- What barriers might prevent me from improving my study habits?
- What could I do to overcome these barriers?
- What are the three things I will do immediately?

This chapter has explored some important learning skills. But it has also stressed that these alone are not enough to ensure you become a powerful learner. The next chapter goes on to introduce one of the most important techniques for learning at work – reflection.

6 The reflective learner

Increasingly, we are becoming aware of just how important it is to be able to learn from practice – from what we do in our working lives. To be an effective learner you need to be well equipped to make the most of the wealth of opportunities for learning in the workplace as described in Chapter 2. You also need to be able to cope with the increasing pace of change and the increasing levels of uncertainty and ambiguity that you encounter at work. And you need to be able to look critically at your practice and at the way things are done at work, and, where relevant, be prepared to promote change.

One of the most crucial ways you can do this is through reflection – the ability to recognise, own and act on your learning from experience.

The chapter explores:

▓ Why reflect? – this section discusses why reflection is important as a means for learning from experience, bridging the gap between theory and practice, coping with ambiguity and change, and developing critical awareness.

▓ Reflective learners: experiment and intuition – this section discusses some aspects of reflection, including how successful professionals conduct experiments to learn from new and potentially difficult situations, the importance of feelings, intuition and critical awareness in reflection, and the value of reflecting with other people.

■ Tools for reflection – this section describes some practical techniques for making reflection effective, including methods for identifying significant experiences, techniques for recording reflection such as learning logs or diaries, and structured models of reflection.

Why reflect?

Reflection is something we all do, to a certain extent at least. Jean Piaget found that reflection was one of the advanced thinking skills that adolescents develop as they approach adulthood. Whenever you stand back and look critically at something you are doing you are reflecting on your practice. As Mary Fitzgerald (1994) has put it, it is through reflection that we are able 'to critically analyse and interpret' our own work. We may reflect during an activity – 'reflection *in* action' – or we may do it after the event – 'reflection *on* action'.

We now look in more detail at some of the reasons why developing the ability to reflect is potentially valuable.

Reflection is crucial to learning from experience

As we saw in Chapter 2, the workplace offers a wide range of opportunities for learning. However, these opportunities do not necessarily lead to learning – many slip past unnoticed. Research into learning from experience suggests that it is reflection that enables the effective learner to recognise these opportunities when they happen, and learn from them.

Research into learning from experience suggests that it is reflection that enables the effective learner to recognise opportunities when they happen, and learn from them.

In his book *Experiential Learning: Experience as a Source of Learning and Development* David Kolb acknowledges a major debt to the ideas of the 'gestalt' psychologist Kurt Lewin. Lewin had argued that reflection on experience provides the basis for forming more abstract ideas which can then be applied and tested in further experience. To illustrate this, Kolb presented reflective learning as a cycle (see Figure 6.1)

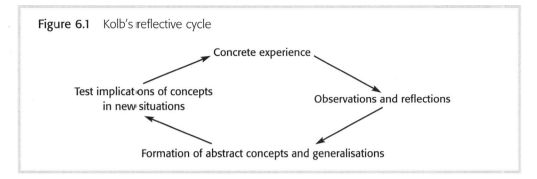

Figure 6.1   Kolb's reflective cycle

This model, which Kolb labelled 'the Lewinian Experiential Learning Model', has entered the folklore as 'the Kolb cycle', despite the fact that Kolb himself rejected the idea that the learning process is a closed loop.

Reflection

John worked with a group of supervisors who were developing their team leadership skills. One supervisor had recently taken on a new team, and had run into a number of problems – for example, if a member of the team was off sick, other members of the team were not readily able to stand in for them. The supervisor's initial reaction was to question the ability of individual team members. Reflecting more deeply on the issue led her to realise that the problem stemmed from a lack of clear procedures. As the team started to record the way they did things they were able to build this into a manual of procedures. They could then use this if a member of staff was away or sick, and to help to brief new people.

Reflection can help to bridge the gap between theory and practice

Traditionally, much learning has taken place off the job, before someone is expected to do the work. However, during our research work we have encountered many people who are conscious of the problems in applying this off-job learning to the workplace. They argue that a person cannot necessarily do a job just because they have learned the required knowledge or skills – they need to know how to apply this knowledge or skills to real work problems. Reflecting on the real work problems can help you to identify how best to apply what you know in practice.

New skills

In recent years there has been a trend towards multiskilling in engineering – engineers who were specialists in, say, mechanical engineering, are being asked to acquire skills in, say, electrical engineering. This raises issues around how best people can learn these new skills. For example, we met people from one engineering firm who had visited – as part of a benchmarking exercise – a plant which had sought to develop new skills through an off-the-job pro-gramme. The programme had experienced problems because, once the maintenance staff returned to the shop floor, they had problems applying their new skills. Our contacts were determined that their own engineers should learn as much as possible on the shop floor – and this was likely to require an important element of reflection on the new practices.

Reflection can help deal with ambiguity, stress and change

Managers and professionals face increasing stress and pressure at work. These pressures result, in particular, from increased workload, from the pace of change, and from the increasing need to work closely with and involve customers and clients. As a result, we often have to cope with new, unique problems we have not met before. The ability to reflect is essential to recognising and confronting the uncertainty we feel as we try to deal with these problems.

Reflection leads to critical awareness

Reflection enables us to look critically at our own behaviour, the behaviour of other people, and at the organisational and social context within which we operate. Reflecting on our own behaviour can help us to develop our self-awareness, while reflecting on what goes on around us can help us to become aware of problems and things that need to change.

Critical awareness

One occupational group facing these issues are care assistants, who play an increasingly important role in caring for people in care homes and the community. The care sector vocational standards seek to define certain standards of behaviour in care through what they call a 'value base'. During our research work we met care assistants who are actively using this value base for reflecting on their own conduct and on the performance of others. For example, one care assistant told us:

'Last week one of the other care assistants suggested to me that I hadn't handled a situation quite the right way. We had a chat about what I should have done. I thought that was great – it wouldn't have happened before.'

All this means that, while reflection is crucial to learning from work, it is not a bland or innocuous process – it is central to becoming a powerful, critical learner who is prepared to challenge the way things are done. When Donald Schön, one of the most influential thinkers about reflection, began his research, he did so in direct challenge to what he saw as the predominant 'technical rationality' which suggested that professionals could solve problems by following the rules they learnt in their professional education. For Schön (1983), this view places us under great stress – we are seen as an 'expert' who 'is presumed to know, and must claim to do so' regardless of our own uncertainty.

Schön believed that the problems we face are more complex than this. Very often the problem contains a unique set of circumstances and as a result we are 'not the only one in the situation to have relevant and important knowledge' – both our own uncertainties, and our knowledge of other people involved, are relevant to solving the problem. This leads to an important change both in the way we see ourselves and the way we relate to other people.

The critical theorists who we met in Chapter 4 go even further. Jurgen Habermas argues that critical reflection can uncover 'the traces of violence that deform repeated attempts at dialogue and recurrently close off the path to unconstrained communication'. Critical reflection is therefore essential to becoming free, autonomous and responsible people.

John Fowler and Mel Chevannes (1998) have described reflection as an 'emancipatory' process for many professionals, and Marsick has defined the reflective learner as:

A learner who is continually sensitive to why things are being done in a certain way, and the discrepancies that exist between what is being said and what is being done.

Learning in the Workplace (Marsick, 1987)

It follows that reflection is not always easy. One student teacher, describing the experience of keeping a reflective diary during teaching practice, commented that reflection is not the safe option:

It seems to be much safer and secure not to reflect, because I don't have to change that which I don't see as wrong.

'Reflection and professional education: art, science and competency' (Saylor, 1990)

All this suggests that reflection is both a challenging and rewarding activity.

Reflective learners: experiment and intuition

So what makes someone a reflective learner? A number of writers and researchers have explored the topic and this section brings together some of the most useful insights into what is involved, including:

- The idea that reflection involves applying the principles of **scientific enquiry** to our work.

- The importance of **feelings, intuition and critical thinking** in reflection.

- The scope for **reflecting with other people**.

Reflection as scientific enquiry

The starting point for any discussion of reflection has to be the work of Donald Schön. In his book *The Reflective Practitioner* Schön (1983) explores how professionals and managers use reflection to help them approach and tackle the often very complex problems they encounter in their work. Schön concludes that, when faced with a new problem, professionals become 'researchers in the practice context' – indeed, they conduct real world experiments to try to solve the problem.

Schön calls this creative and artistic approach to problems 'reflection in action'. In this, Schön is echoing some of the ideas of George Kelly, who argued that the way in which people interpret the world parallels the process of scientific enquiry, and that 'behaviour is an experiment'.

Schön avoids giving a simple recipe for reflection in action as he believes the process is complex and varied. For example, the way a manager reflects on a problem for which he or she needs an immediate solution will be different from the way he or she tackles longer term issues. However, Schön does describe some of the main things that professionals seem to do when they tackle problems. When they first approach a new problem:

- They allow themselves to experience 'surprise, puzzlement or confusion'. This may simply be a feeling or anxiety that something is wrong, or an awareness that they have not encountered or read about this before. They accept that, while these feelings may be unsettling, they are essential to the process of continually improving what they do.

- They reflect critically on the problem before them. They reflect on the facts as they know them, the relationships involved, their own feelings. They are prepared to look critically at their own assumptions and at accepted ways of tackling this kind of problem.

- They may then 'reframe' the situation – they may come up with a new theory or hypothesis about the problem, and test this out through an experiment.

Eye-to-eye with the unexpected

Schön gives as an example an eye specialist who is confronted with a patient who has two eye conditions at the same time – an inflammation and a glaucoma – both of which appear to be getting worse. The specialist has never met this combination of conditions before, and is initially puzzled about what to do. After initial reflection, he hypothesises that the treatment for each condition is aggravating the other condition. He conducts an experiment to test this out, by temporarily withholding all treatments to see what effect this will have. As a result the glaucoma disappears, proving the hypothesis that it was caused by the treatment for the inflammation. The specialist is then able to consider other ways of treating the inflammation.

Schön also believes that it is possible to develop some of the skills of reflection after an event, through what he calls 'reflection on action'. This process may be supported by another skilled person.

The importance of feelings in reflection

The idea that reflection must take account of feelings is taken further by David Boud and colleagues in their book *Reflection: Turning Experience into Learning*. They argue that, after an initial reflection to any experience, it is crucial to 'attend to feelings'. This involves:

- Making the most of any positive feelings about the experience.

- 'Discharging' negative feelings, either by writing them down or discussing them with a trusted person.

Recognising and exploring feelings like this makes it possible to evaluate the experience as an opportunity for learning.

The importance of intuition in reflection

In her book *From Novice to Expert*, Patricia Benner, drawing on her research with nurses, has described a five-stage model of skill acquisition that people go through as they become more experienced in any role (see Figure 6.2).

At the novice stage the individual is a newcomer who has just started work in a new role. The novice will tend to rely on the rules they have learnt, and seek to apply these to their new experiences in a relatively inflexible way. As they gain greater experience of the work, they are able to progress through competency, proficiency and eventually to become

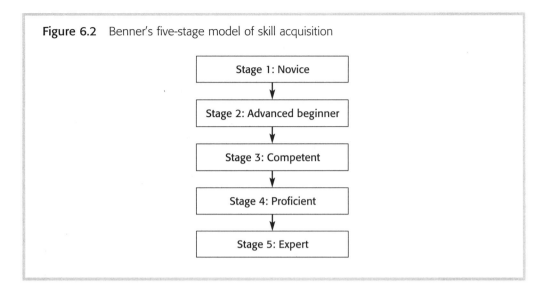

Figure 6.2   Benner's five-stage model of skill acquisition

expert in their field. In the process they become less dependent on the rules and more able to draw on their own experience.

In some ways Benner's findings echo those of Schön. However, her ideas place additional emphasis on the role of intuition which she defines as 'understanding without a rationale' (Benner and Tanner, 1987). She argues that 'detached, reflective thinking' must be balanced by intuitive, creative thinking which includes 'the vague feelings, hunches or sense that something is not right'. And she offers some insights into how experts apply such intuitive thinking in practice:

◼ They increasingly come to rely on their own concrete experience as they tackle problems. They recognise similarities with – and differences from – previous problems they have tackled without jumping to the conclusion that similar problems are identical.

◼ They are increasingly able to look at a situation as a complete whole, and within this to identify those factors that stand out as being especially relevant.

> They move from being 'detached observers' towards being 'involved performers'. They are able to tune in to their clients and seek to understand their background.

This emphasis on intuition provides an important addition to our understanding of reflection. Benner's work has proved highly influential in nursing where people have long suspected that intuitive knowledge is a crucial ingredient in caring. However it has much wider relevance – it is also crucial for managers and other professionals to be able to recognise their intuition and the ways they can use it in their reflective practice.

The importance of a critical perspective

Another important addition to our understanding is critical reflection. Schön, of course, recognises that reflection must involve the ability to think critically and question assumptions. However, while reflection in action leads to learning about our work, and how best to tackle it, critical reflection leads to learning about why the work is being done, and the broader social and organisational context.

This perspective on reflection comes from critical theory which we introduced in Chapter 4. Paulo Freire used critical reflection in his work directing government literacy programmes in Brazil and later Chile. These programmes brought illiterate peasants together in 'culture circles' and led to thousands of people learning to read. Freire's method was not, however, restricted purely to helping people to read and write – it also encouraged people to become aware of the reasons why they were illiterate in the first place, and their relative powerlessness in their society.

Critical reflection is also used by professionals to deepen their awareness of the factors and constraints that influence their role, the roles of their colleagues and the social context of their clients. There are three processes at work here:

> Becoming aware of factors in the organisation and the wider social structure that act as barriers to communication and constraints on our action – the process of *enlightenment*. This involves:
> — questioning assumptions about what we know and how we

know it – what Freire calls 'conventional explanations of reality'
— challenging beliefs, rules and traditions that are accepted without question
— asking whose interests are served by the beliefs, rules and traditions
— discovering how we may actually reinforce these beliefs, rules and traditions.

Becoming aware of our own ability to influence and change our own situations – the process of *empowerment*.

Taking action to remove the barriers to communication and constraints on action – the process of *emancipation*.

Critical reflection can therefore be a powerful tool that can be used to give us a broader picture of our role. Linda Wilson-Thomas (1995) argues that critical reflection can help professionals to become 'ethical, moral, responsible and accountable individuals'.

The value of reflecting together

While reflection is a valuable individual activity, it can also be useful to reflect with other people. This may take the form of:

Reflection in pairs, where two people take turns to share their experiences with a partner.

Reflection in small groups, where people describe their experiences and ask for feedback from the other members of the group.

The principal benefit of reflecting with a partner or a group is the scope it provides for personal support and feedback. In addition, it can help to provide a structure for reflection, and an example to learn from.

Within a number of occupations – in particular health, education and social work – people have recently started to examine ways in which reflection like this can become more formally built into professional development. One model that has become widely used is a process called clinical supervision, defined by the NHS Executive in 1993 as:

A formal process of professional support and learning which enables individual practitioners to develop knowledge and competence, assume responsibility for their own practice and enhance consumer protection and safety of care in complex clinical situations.

Clinical supervision involves regular meetings between two individuals or a small group where professionals describe important recent experiences from their work. Together, the participants reflect on these experiences, consider alternative ways of tackling them, and discuss what they have learned from them. They are then able to apply what they learn back at work.

While learning through reflection is a prime objective of clinical supervision, the process is also designed to raise organisational standards for quality, and to provide support to individuals in situations of stress.

Reflection in clinical supervision in East Somerset

The East Somerset NHS Trust is one of the many NHS organisations to adopt a system of clinical supervision. Initiated in 1995, clinical supervision is aimed at nurses, midwives and health visitors and provides an opportunity for professionals to share their knowledge, skills and experiences in an environment of trust, mutual support and confidentiality.

The aims of the approach are to:

- encourage the development of professional expertise through reflective practice
- encourage learning from each other
- celebrate examples of good practice
- improve communication and build confidence and self-esteem
- investigate alternative models of managing care scenarios when difficulties have been experienced
- improve performance and clinical effectiveness.

Most supervision takes place in groups, although individual supervision can be used if special circumstances require it. Members of staff are trained to become facilitators of group sessions.

At the start of each session the group identifies issues for reflection, such as:

- an example of good practice
- a critical incident
- conflicts in care delivery
- personal difficulties and stresses
- interpersonal relationships within the care team.

Clinical supervision operates entirely outside the line management system. All issues raised in group sessions are completely confidential and cannot be used for disciplinary measures.

Bringing these ideas together

So far, this chapter has described a range of ideas and insights into reflection. But how can you apply these in practice? We look at this in the final section of this chapter – 'Tools for reflection'. But first we close this section by picking out some of the most important ingredients of reflective practice:

- **Recognising triggers for reflection**. If you are to reflect on what you do, you need to identify the signs that reflection may be valuable. We can call these signs 'triggers for reflection'. Triggers for reflection could include:
  — feeling uneasy about something without quite knowing why
  — feeling that your existing knowledge is not appropriate to a new context
  — having to do something new or different
  — something going wrong – or indeed right
  — not knowing or being certain about what to do
  — recognising that an episode – perhaps a series of connected events – has been completed.

  One way of identifying triggers for reflection is the critical incident technique, which we describe in the last section of this chapter 'Tools for reflection'.

Learning to accept and explore uncertainty. It is common to experience feelings of uncertainty – for example, being vaguely aware that there will be problems with a project in the future. It is also common to suppress these feelings in the hope that they will go away. The 'Tools for reflection' offer some models you can use to take your thinking forward when you experience uncertainty –the model of structured reflection may be particularly useful.

Creating time for reflection. As you become more experienced at reflection, you will become better at reflecting on problems while you are dealing with them – this is very much what Schön means by 'reflection *in* action'. Before you reach this stage – and indeed after you do so – you need to take time to reflect on what has happened after the event – 'reflection *on* action'. This means allowing a little time each day or week which you will spend quietly thinking through recent events. This could be time spent quietly at home or at work – or it might be time spent walking, cycling or driving. You could use another of the 'Tools for reflection' – the reflective cycle – as a basis for this.

Recording your reflection. It can make sense to write down your thoughts and feelings about the episode, using, for example, reflective diaries, learning logs or structured reflection as described in the 'Tools for reflection'.

Using creative and intuitive techniques. For example, brainstorming, mind-mapping or drawing a problem – these are described in Chapter 7.

Reflecting with another person or people. The clinical supervision model described above is a formal approach to shared reflection in an organisation. However, there is no reason why you should not work informally with a partner or a small group in a very similar way. You could, for example, meet regularly (say, once a month) with a friend or colleague and describe one or more key events that you have experienced over that time. Again, you could use the reflective cycle as a basis for this. Chapter 9 looks at learning together in more detail.

▨ **Having the courage to challenge ways of doing things**. Being able to think critically and to challenge assumptions is also crucial – see Chapter 8 on the value of critical questioning.

Tools for reflection

Before looking at ways of improving your reflection skills it is helpful to assess your current strengths and weaknesses. Table 6.1 covers those most important ingredients of reflective practice detailed in the previous section. There are several tools and techniques you can use to develop your ability to reflect. We close this chapter by discussing:

Table 6.1   A self-assessment grid for reflection skills

How good are you at:	I can do this	I need to develop this
1 Recognising triggers for reflection		
2 Learning to accept and explore uncertainty		
3 Creating time for reflection		
4 Recording your reflection		
5 Using creative and intuitive techniques		
6 Reflecting with another person or people		
7 Challenging ways of doing things		

▨   identifying significant experiences for reflection

▨   keeping a reflective diary

▨   keeping learning logs

▨   using structured reflection

▨   using a reflective cycle.

Identifying significant experiences for reflection

For reflection to be successful, it is clearly important to reflect on significant experiences. This raises the question of what constitutes a significant experience.

One way of doing this it to use the concept introduced in Chapter 1 of 'episode analysis'. Harré and Secord have defined an episode as any experience which is both *complete* and *meaningful* to the participant.

So an episode could be relatively short – for instance, a project meeting or a single client contact. Or it could be much longer – for example, a series of contacts with a client or a complete project. The crucial thing is that you feel that this adds up to a meaningful episode.

Another useful concept is that of 'critical incident analysis', originally proposed by Flanagan. Critical incident analysis was designed for use in research – Flanagan developed it in his research with airline pilots and it has also been adopted in nursing research, notably by Patricia Benner. However, within research it is used as a way of helping participants to reflect on the important parts of their work, and so it is potentially useful as a tool for identifying significant experiences.

Identifying critical incidents

A critical incident could be any experience at work – including very ordinary or typical events – that, for example:

- went unusually well
- went badly or led to problems
- you found especially demanding or challenging
- made a real difference in your work
- captured the essence of what your job is about.

Keeping a reflective diary

One of the most widely used tools for reflection is the reflective diary. A reflective diary is a journal in which you record your most important experiences each day, how you felt about them, and what you have learnt from them.

Our research certainly suggests that some people, at least, find it particularly helpful to write about their experiences. As part of one project we carried out, we asked a range of young people to talk to us about their experience of reflection and carrying out self-evaluations. For example, a university student told us:

Writing things down is the major benefit. The act of reflecting is more important than anything.

Reflective diaries can be very personal things, and it is important to adopt a format and approach which suits your personal style and which helps you to learn. The example below suggests some questions to consider when planning a diary.

Planning a reflective diary

1   Choose a format – a book or a file with individual sheets? What size paper?

2   Plan how you will make entries – will they be entirely open-ended, or might you use some questions to guide your reflection?

3   How will you distinguish description from reflection? – by using two columns, or facing pages?

4   Decide how often to make entries – at regular intervals – for example, daily or weekly? Or after significant events? Or after the episode has been completed?

5   Decide when and where will be the best time to complete the diary – in the evening, or first thing in the morning? At work or at home?

6   Find ways of getting started – if you find it hard to start writing, begin with some description, or jotting down ideas as they come to you.

Yvonne L'Aiguille, a senior sister in the Oxford Radcliffe Hospital, has described how she uses a reflective diary to 'record the highs and lows' of her working life. She aims to make entries once or twice a week, and finds that it is important to choose the right time and place:

'I find that to write effectively in my journal I like to be physically comfortable. I have a bath, get a cup of tea and then take myself upstairs where I will be guaranteed peace and quiet.'

Yvonne uses an A4 book, and writes her descriptions on the left hand page and her reflection and analysis on the right hand page. Sometimes she writes in connected prose, other times she makes notes and links thoughts together with lines and doodles.

Yvonne is conscious that she finds it easier to reflect on positive experiences than on negative ones, and that she could possibly reflect formally on her work more often. She also finds it easier to reflect with another person rather than to write down her reflections. Nonetheless, she has found her journal beneficial – she comments that, as her skills of reflection improve, she becomes better able to put them into practice during her work – to 'reflect-in-action'.

Adapted from: 'Pushing back the boundaries of personal experience' (L'Aiguille, 1994)

Keeping learning logs

An alternative model for recording reflection is the learning log advocated by Greene and Gibbons. A learning log is a sheet of paper designed as a form which you can use to structure your writing about significant experiences. Typically, a learning log will have spaces to describe:

- the experience itself

- your conclusions about it

- any actions you plan to take as a result.

You can store learning log entries in a file – this has the added advantage that you can classify and link entries together. The example below shows a sample learning log.

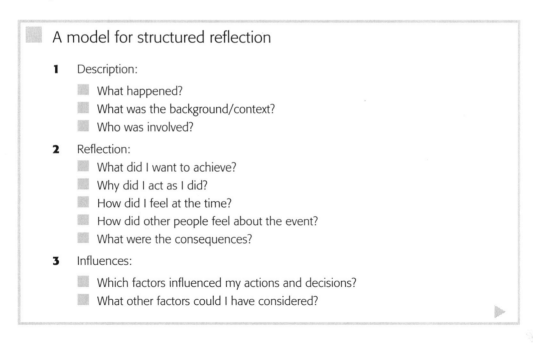

Learning log format

Date:
What happened:

What you have learnt from this:

What you will do as a result: By when:

Using structured reflection

For many people a relatively unstructured, open-ended approach to diary keeping is perfectly acceptable. However, other people like to use a more structured approach. Several writers (e.g. Johns, 1992) have described models of structured reflection – they generally involve answering a number of questions about an event, as in the following example.

A model for structured reflection

1 Description:
  - What happened?
  - What was the background/context?
  - Who was involved?

2 Reflection:
  - What did I want to achieve?
  - Why did I act as I did?
  - How did I feel at the time?
  - How did other people feel about the event?
  - What were the consequences?

3 Influences:
  - Which factors influenced my actions and decisions?
  - What other factors could I have considered?

4   Alternatives:

■ What else could I have done?

■ What difference might these alternative actions have made?

5   Learning:

■ What have I learnt from the event?

■ How has the event changed me?

■ If this happened again, what would I do?

Using a reflective cycle

If you reflect with another person or people you may find that the structured model for reflection is too complex to form the basis for discussion. One alternative is to consider the questions as a series of activities that make up a dynamic cycle, drawing on the learning cycle we discussed at

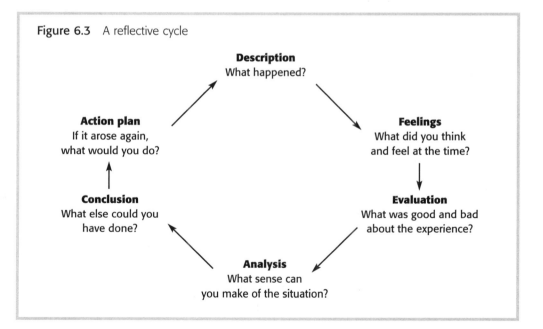

Figure 6.3   A reflective cycle

Description
What happened?

Feelings
What did you think
and feel at the time?

Evaluation
What was good and bad
about the experience?

Analysis
What sense can
you make of the situation?

Conclusion
What else could you
have done?

Action plan
If it arose again,
what would you do?

the start of this chapter. The cycle in Figure 6.3 is adapted from Graham Gibbs (1988).

There are other aspects of reflection that we mentioned earlier in this chapter – the need to be creative, the need to think critically and the value of reflecting together. The chapters that follow explore these aspects in more detail – beginning in the next chapter with creativity.

7 The creative learner

> We must change the concept of creativity from being something that is 'added on' to education, skills, training and management and make sure it becomes intrinsic to all of these.
>
> Chris Smith MP, Secretary of State for Culture, Media and Sport

Many people associate creativity primarily with the arts – music, drama, dance, literature and so on. These are often known as 'the creative arts' in contrast to the sciences which tend to be thought of as uncreative. But creativity is not unique to the arts – it is also fundamental to advances in science, technology, politics or any arena.

> There are few areas of life where the nation's priorities for health, education, employment and industry are not dependent on the development and application of creative, practical skills.
>
> *Learning through making: A national enquiry into the value of creative, practical education*
> (Crafts Council, 1998)

Creativity is indeed possible in all areas of human activity be it work, play, leisure or any aspect of daily life. Learning and creativity are very closely intertwined; creative effort results from, and contributes to, learning and each of us can improve our creativity by combining human creative potential with the power of learning.

This chapter explores the following topics:

- We are all creative.
- Creativity: making the future.
- Using creativity in your learning.
- Learning to be creative.

We are all creative

We sometimes talk as if it is only very rare and exceptional people who have the luck to be creative. We think of great men and women who have made ground breaking discoveries, created great paintings or written important books. Often they seem to have achieved these things with little or no help – we assume they were simply brilliant individuals with an inborn creative talent or gift. If this is the case then there seems little point in developing people's creativity – you've either got it or you haven't!

We do not believe this. In our view we are all born with the capacity to be creative and every one of us can develop and improve our creativity. In other words, we see creativity as a fundamental human power – and one that is very closely related to the power of learning.

This view is summed up very neatly in the 'democratic concept of creativity' proposed in *All Our Futures*, the report of the National Advisory Committee on Creative and Cultural Education which:

. . . recognises the potential for creative achievement in all fields of human activity, and the capacity for such achievements in the many and not the few.

The comedian Lenny Henry brings the two viewpoints together:

There are people in the world who have to create to live – it's just something they have to do. There are others who live to create . . . . And then there are people (most of us I think) who are creative, but don't know what to do with it – how to use it. I think these people could be nudged in the right direction by teachers.

Quoted in: All Our Futures (NACCCE, 1999)

How creativity works

There are two main schools of thought on how creativity works:

- The *association* of parts of problems.
- *Restructuring* of wholes.

Association

This approach sees thinking as a chain of ideas and creativity as the pairing of 'remote' ideas – ones which are less likely to be associated in people's minds. An example is likening a lion's head to a chrysanthemum flower. The combination of flowers and ferocity may seem incongruous but the image generated is vivid and appealing.

Restructuring

The structuralist approach to creativity is about seeing the whole and then re-arranging it from existing ideas and knowledge. It involves dividing a problem into sub-wholes with clear reference to the whole: the argument is that creative solutions come from changing the point of reference.

Another structural view was provided by Sigmund Freud. He believed that conflict gives birth to creativity. Thus while the creative person resolves conflicts fruitfully and brings new resolutions to old problems, neurotics maintain their delusions. Freud's approach emphasises symbols, dreams and mental fantasies rather than reasoning.

A synthesis

Both the associative and structuralist perspectives have value and apply to different situations. Many researchers have concluded that creative thinking involves both thinking broadly (or generatively) when generating lots of possible ideas and then narrowly (or critically) when homing in on a particular idea or solution.

Convergent and divergent thinking

There are clear links between these two approaches to creativity and the notion of convergent and divergent thinking.

The concept of convergent and divergent thinking arises from the work of Getzels and Jackson in the 1960s. These two psychologists believed that the conventional intelligence tests of the time were too narrow. They were particularly critical of the way in which tests invited only one answer – encouraging people to 'converge' on a specific response. As a result Getzels and Jackson argued that these tests did not tap into people's creativity. They devised open-ended tests which encouraged people to come up with as many answers as possible. They called these 'divergent' questions because they encouraged people to diverge from the original question. The best known example of this type of question is 'How many uses can you think of for a brick?'

In his books *Contrary Imaginations* and *Frames of Mind*, Liam Hudson built on the work of Getzels and Jackson and found that people who specialised in the arts and social sciences tended to score higher on divergent tests than conventional IQ tests and that the results for people specialising in science were the other way round. However, the largest group were all-rounders, scoring high on both tests. Hudson concluded that you cannot identify creativity with divergent thinking because people who test as convergent thinkers are often also very creative – for instance, finding new and original solutions to classic problems in mathematics.

The tendency to equate creativity with divergent thinking is now strongly questioned and it is generally agreed that both ways of looking at a problem are relevant to creativity. It is recognised that the process may involve using divergent approaches to generate ideas and then using more analytical convergent processes to sift and evaluate the ideas. The ideas are then developed using either or both convergent or divergent methods.

Characteristics of the creative process

There are four characteristics of the creative process:

- It involves thinking and behaving *imaginatively.*

- The imaginative activity is *purposeful* – it is directed towards achieving an objective.

- The activity generates something *original.*

- The outcome must be of *value.*

Adapted from: All Our Futures (NACCCE, 1999)

Judging creativity

So, if creativity can be seen as:

Imaginative activity fashioned so as to produce outcomes that are both original and of value.

Quoted in: All Our Futures (NACCCE, 1999)

. . . how can we judge what is and is not creative and how do we know that an idea is truly original or of value? People applying for patents, for example, must certainly believe that what they have produced is the result of creative effort.

Patently creative

The criteria used by the US Patents Office to determine whether or not a product is worthy of a patent are that the product:

- must have come about as a result of qualified intellectual activity, but it should be clear that it has resulted from something other than logic

- must be useful and provide a stride forward

- must overcome special difficulties

- is considered particularly creative if experts have been sceptical about its success.

Originality is the most commonly used criterion in creativity research, but we should be wary of using originality as the basis for our judgements. While creative ideas are virtually always unusual, novel or unique, original ideas may be so because they are worthless or unrealistic. Ronald Finke has developed the concept of 'creative realism' which aims to ensure ideas which are **both** creative and realistic (see Figure 7.1).

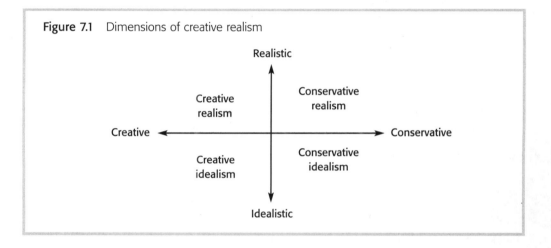

Figure 7.1   Dimensions of creative realism

Let's look at these dimensions in more detail:

- **Conservative realism** ties in with established, traditional ideas. It is very structural and low on imagination and divergence. Creative realists tend to avoid ambiguity and uncertainty.

- **Creative idealism** is associated with what might be called 'crackpot' ideas. These trains of thought are original, but often fanciful and unrealistic.

- **Conservative idealism** is the extension of common ideas that were unrealistic to begin with, e.g. women are inferior to men. These ideas are likely to be unimaginative with no basis in fact and are often used to close down innovative thinking.

■ **Creative realism** shows imagination and divergence but is connected to real issues and concepts.

Creative people

While we are all naturally creative, some of us may have had our creativity educated out of us or have been inhibited by the kinds of experiences which can stifle creativity. Creativity has been described as the public expression of imagination, which is essentially private. However, imagination has not always been highly regarded by society or by teachers. For centuries the ability to imagine has been the subject of discrimination, suspicion, even hatred.

Self-image and creativity

In 1962, McKinnon carried out research with trainee architects to find out how people would describe themselves in terms of creativity. He divided them into two groups on the basis of creativity tests and their teachers' opinions. One group was labelled 'creative' and the other less so.

■ He found that the 'creative' group described themselves more frequently as inventive, determined, independent, individualistic, enthusiastic and industrious.

■ The 'less creative' group described themselves more often as responsible, sincere, reliable, dependable, clear thinking, tolerant and understanding.

A number of studies have been carried out to identify behaviours of creative people. These characteristics do not describe an individual – no one person is likely to have all these features, but an especially creative person is likely to have more of them than a less creative person. The following example suggests how you can use these to assess your creative potential.

Assess your creative potential

Look through the following characteristics of creative people. Assess yourself against each characteristic using the following scale:

'Not me at all'	Score 1
'Partly me; I have some of this quality.'	Score 2
'Definitely me'	Score 3

Score

- I like to do my own planning and make my own decisions. ☐
- I have less need of other people and seldom ask peers or teachers for their opinion. ☐
- I am optimistic when presented with complex, difficult tasks. ☐
- I have a lot of ideas – some of which provoke ridicule. ☐
- I am curious, questioning and constructively critical. ☐
- I make less of a distinction between work and play. ☐
- I am more likely to stand my ground in the face of criticism. ☐
- I can tolerate uncertainty and ambiguity better than most. ☐
- I am not necessarily one of the 'best' students. ☐
- I am more original and flexible. ☐
- I am independent, autonomous and self-disciplined. ☐
- I am thorough, persevere and have a liking and capacity for work. ☐
- I reject repression and am less inhibited, formal and conventional. ☐
- I am sensitive and in touch with and able to express emotions without embarrassment. ☐
- I am often attracted to the unknown, not frightened of it. ☐

Add up your total score – no one should expect to get the maximum of 45, because, as we've said, the list does not add up to a whole person. But if you've scored over 30, then you probably possess many creative attributes. However, you should now look back at your scores and ask yourself the following questions:

▶

> **What are my creative strengths?** – the characteristics for which I scored 3. Is there a pattern, what do they say about my approach to creativity?
>
> **For which characteristics did I score 1?** What might be getting in the way of my creativity? Are these aspects of myself I would like to develop? (It's OK, and sometimes right, to answer 'No' to this question!)
>
> **Have I given myself 2 for a lot of characteristics?** What does this imply?

Obstacles to creativity

One of the most justifiable charges that can be levelled against our education system is that it has neglected, and all too often suppressed, the natural creativity of the young.

The Art and Science of Creativity (Kneller, 1965)

There is so much which can get in the way of our creativity, and fear is probably the greatest barrier – fear of failing, fear of other's opinions, fear of the unknown. The following obstacles can be either internally or externally imposed:

There is so much which can get in the way of our creativity, and fear is probably the greatest barrier.

- Pressures to conform.

- Ridicule of unusual ideas.

- Fear of the change that might result from the ideas.

- Excessive quest for success – and its rewards.

- Emphasis on certainty – only one answer will do and it's got to be perfect.

- Intolerance of a playful attitude – creativity is fun!

How managers block creativity

The American, Chris Argyris, carried out some of the most influential research with middle managers (1985). He found that they stifled innovation from their subordinates by:

- Not listening or paying attention to ideas and suggestions.
- Undermining ideas from the top by failing to show enthusiasm or commitment.
- Acting defensively, refusing to stick their necks out.

Perhaps the most worrying thing was that Argyris found that these managers were quite unaware that they were acting in this way.

And the culture within organisations and pressures on professionals often deter creativity.

Perhaps the emphasis on accountability gives no margin for error – but if there's no margin for error how do you learn? How do we make space for that in the culture of responsibility, professionalism and accountability?

School improvement adviser

How managers can encourage creativity

Managers in organisations can play a key role in encouraging, harnessing and developing creativity through the following strategies:

- Listening to staff and valuing their ideas.
- Delegating without over-directing or providing excessive guidance.
- Allowing the chance to fail intelligently.
- 'Let the boat rock' – being prepared to consider radical ideas which challenge the status quo.
- Showing a positive attitude to change.

Creativity: making the future

Creative thinking is the raw material of innovation – and companies must innovate if they are to succeed in today's changeable global marketplace . . . A firm needs everyone, at every level to be thinking creatively.

Simon Majaro, Cranfield University

Who needs to be creative?

As we enter the next century creativity is likely to be high on the agenda. Recognising, valuing, developing and harnessing creativity is likely to become increasingly important to individuals, organisations, countries and indeed to the whole human race.

Individuals

When a person finds their creative strengths it can have an enormous impact on self-esteem and on overall achievement. You also need to be creative because it's going to be increasingly valued by employers and other organisations. It's what can make the difference between a competent employee and one who is exceptional.

In Britain, employment in creative industries has grown by 34 per cent in a decade against a background of almost no growth in employment in the economy as a whole.

The most important developments in civilisation have come through the creative process, but ironically, most people have not been taught to create.

The Path of Least Resistance (Fritz, 1994)

Industry

Ideas are the building blocks of innovation and innovation builds industries. Creativity provides the foundation of a new generation of high-tech, high skills industries.

The post-management corporation will be more creative. It used to be assumed that creative individuals should go into the arts, the media, academia or, if forced, into something commercial, then into PR, advertising, or small business rather than into mainstream corporations. This assumption, correct even today, will become outdated.

The Creative Engineer: The Art of Inventing (Kock, 1978)

Countries

Creativity has a huge impact on national income and developing creative abilities is fundamental in meeting the challenge of economic development. New ideas, innovation, and ingenuity in the development of products and services are vital to the competitiveness of countries as well as companies.

Of all the capabilities, creativity is probably the one most likely to vouchsafe our economic growth and our ranking in the league table of world economies.

Professor Stephen Heppel, a member of the Standards Task Force and the Creative Industries Task Force

As global economies change, the demand for creative resources throughout business and industry will increase. This is exemplified by a review of the education system and economy in Japan carried out by the industry federation *Keizai Doyukai*.

Review of Japan's education system and economy

Japan's industry federation, Keizai Doyukai, were concerned that the country had lost the innovation and inspiration which had redefined motorcycle design, produced the Sony Walkman and revolutionised the production line approach to manufacturing. Creativity had been the foundation block on which they had built much of their economic success. They concluded that:

The post-war education system in Japan sought to eliminate deviations in students and deliver an equal, uniform, education throughout the land. This was effective in reaching the goal of catching up industrialised nations. Now, however, the nation is in need of highly creative and independent individuals.

Keizai Doyukai, 1999

Humanity

Every breakthrough in civilisation has come about as a result of creativity. Someone has had an idea and has had the determination and commitment to follow it though. We hear a lot about the information explosion; one of the things we need in order to make the best use of all this information is a creativity explosion.

Original thought, and respect for originality of others, must surely lie at the heart, not just of creativity, but also individuality – our only chance of twenty-first century escape from zombie-ness.

Professor Susan Greenfield

Justifying creativity

In 1999 the UK government, through the National Advisory Committee on Creative and Cultural Education, produced a major report, *All Our Futures: Creativity, Culture and Education*. This wide-ranging document puts the case for developing creative and cultural education which, they say, means forms of education that develop young people's capacities for original ideas and action.

It is, however, a sorry state of affairs that the Committee feels they have to justify paying attention to creativity in education. They pose and respond to a number of questions which say a lot about the kinds of concerns and priorities in education in the UK:

- Isn't an emphasis on creativity and culture a distraction from the core concerns of literacy and numeracy?
- How are creative and cultural education relevant to raising academic standards?
- What has this got to do with helping young people get jobs?
- Is this committee a lobby group for the arts?
- Is this a return to the progressive teaching ideas of the 1960s?

There is, of course, one very simple answer to all of these questions – 'No!'

Creativity is fun

Creativity in learning also contributes to the third of the 3three Es – enjoyment. Think about a recent experience where you were called upon to be creative and succeeded. The chances are that you will have found it both satisfying and enjoyable.

This is because of the important links between creativity and play. Carl Jung wrote:

The creation of something new is not accomplished by the intellect alone, but by the play instinct. The creative mind plays with the objects it loves.

Analytical Psychology (Jung, 1965)

Having it on a plate

Richard Feynmann, an international physicist, describes an experience:

I decided I was only going to do things for the fun of it and only that afternoon, as I was taking lunch, some kid threw up a plate in the cafeteria. There was a blue medallion on the plate. As the plate came down it wobbled. It seemed to me that the blue thing went round faster than the wobble and I wondered what the relationship was between the two – I was just playing; no importance at all.

So I played around with equations of motion of rotating things and I found that if the wobble is small, the blue thing goes round twice as fast as the wobble. I tried to figure out why that was, just for the fun of it, and this led me to the similar problems in the spin of an electron and that led me back into quantum electrodynamics which is the problem I'd been working on.

I continued to play with it in this relaxed fashion and it was like letting a cork out of a bottle. Everything just poured out and in very short order I worked out the things for which I later won the Nobel Prize.

Quoted in: All Our Futures (NACCCE, 1999)

Edward De Bono says of play:

The very uselessness of play is its greatest asset. It is the freedom from design or commitment that allows chance to juxtapose things. Vertical thinkers are ashamed to play, but the only shameful thing is the inability to play.

Lateral Thinking (De Bono, 1973)

Fun and laughter at work

Anna and John have worked together for more than 20 years. A large part of their work involves generating creative ideas.

'We have enormous fun when we are faced with a creative challenge – be it starting a new piece of writing or planning an innovative learning programme. We do a lot of brainstorming – and come up with some hilarious suggestions. We can sometimes be quite silly. But this often releases creative energy and we nearly always find that things start to take shape as a result. I think it helps that we know each other so well and are confident we have each other's respect – this makes it easier for us to share more unusual ideas that we might find harder to express with people we know less well.'

Creative activity often involves playing with ideas and trying out possibilities. In any creative process there are likely to be dead ends: ideas and designs that do not work:

Nine out of ten of my experiments fail, and that is considered a pretty good record amongst scientists.

Professor Sir Harold Kroto, Nobel Prize winning chemist

Using creativity in your learning

There are a number of creative techniques you can use to help you learn effectively. If you like, you can see the techniques listed over the next few pages as an extension of the learning toolkit offered in Chapter 5.

A five-stage creativity process

While there are the occasional sudden flashes of inspiration, brilliant insights and so on, for the creative process to result in valuable learning involves persistence and organisation. The sequence below describes the steps involved:

Stage 1: Orientation – pick out or clarify the issue or problem.

Stage 2: Preparation – gather relevant material or information.

Stage 3: Analysis and ideation – seeking possible solutions and generating ideas.

Stage 4: Incubation – a time lag for the mind to synthesize and assimi-
late information and ideas.

Stage 5: Evaluation – putting the pieces together, testing solutions.

Adapted from: *All Our Futures* (NACCCE, 1999)

Creative problem solving

If you think there is only one answer then you will find only one.

Teaching for Effective Learning (Scottish Consultative Council on the Curriculum, 1996)

Problem solving is an area where you will find considerable use for your
creative abilities. Problem solving needs to follow a clear path so that it
makes the best use of creativity within a structured process such as the
one below:

- **Understanding the problem**. Start by being clear about what the
  problem is. Clarify, define, refine, re-define and find out information
  and facts.

- **Generating ideas**. Different types of thinking will generate a range of
  different ideas. Find many options through 'fluent' thinking; a variety of options come from 'flexible' thinking; novel options will
  result from 'original' thinking; detailed or refined options will come
  through 'elaborative' thinking.

- **Evaluating ideas**. Once you have generated as many possible solutions as you can then you should examine, review, cluster and select
  them.

- **Planning for action**. Finally, if the process is to be productive and
  actually solve the problem you identified, you will need to plan
  how to implement your solution. This may involve selling your
  idea to others or thinking about how you might need to overcome
  barriers which stand in the way of change.

Guidelines for creative problem solving

The following guidelines offer an approach to creative problem solving:

- Never accept the first solution you think of – generate a number of possible ideas.
- Be aware of your own defensiveness about the problem – if you feel threatened you are less likely to be creative.
- Get feedback from others less closely involved.
- Think of a solution someone else might have come up with.
- Think of opposites to your solutions.
- Give ideas a chance to 'incubate'.
- Be self-confident – really good ideas frequently involve some personal risk and you may need to be prepared to stick your neck out.
- Remember, weird ideas often spark great ones.

Brainstorming

A central tool for creativity that can be invaluable in problem solving is brainstorming. This is a way of stimulating people to think creatively, to come up with original and alternative ideas. Developed by Alex Osborn in the 1960s, it relies on the postponement of judgement or criticism and aims at generating a large number of ideas, including some which may be genuinely weird.

Brainstorming is often done in a group but can also work for the individual. With a group, however, one person's contribution may spark another's idea and so there is a richer and deeper resource for ideas.

There are four ground rules for brainstorming:

- Criticism of another's ideas (or your own if you're working alone) is forbidden until the ideas session is over.

- All ideas must be acknowledged and considered no matter how irrelevant or ridiculous they seem.

How brainstorming works

1   Focus on the topic – e.g. by writing it on a large piece of paper or a flip-chart if you are working as a group.

2   Tell or remind people of the rules of brainstorming – no criticism or commenting is allowed during the creative phase.

3   Spend some time – say 5–10 minutes – coming up with ideas around the topic. During this creative stage, people should feel free to say anything they like – even silly, rude or ludicrous suggestions may spark off a good idea in someone else's mind.

4   When all ideas are exhausted, move into the evaluation phase. Look over the ideas that have been generated, and decide which to keep and which to reject. In some cases you may wish to organise ideas under headings.

5   Decide what to do as a result.

- The more ideas generated the better.

- Combining and refining ideas is desirable – in groups people should draw on and develop each others' ideas.

You can use brainstorming and other creative techniques such as mind mapping (see Chapter 5) – where you create a spider diagram with lines linking together the ideas you brainstorm – or drawing what you think and feel, whenever you feel the need to think widely or solve a problem.

Lateral thinking

In 1973 Edward De Bono published his book on lateral thinking. This was one of the first books about our mental processes to become popular and reach outside the academic community.

De Bono contrasts lateral thinkers, who explore all ways of looking at a topic, with vertical thinkers who stick to what they consider reasonable and logical.

He explains how he came up with these two descriptors:

It is not possible to dig a hole in a different place by digging the same hole deeper.

He describes lateral thinking as taking a completely new position and then working backwards to try and construct a logical path between this new position and the starting point.

Principles for lateral thinking

- Recognise dominant or polarising ideas which can get in the way of free thought.
- Get rid of dominating ideas by, for example, exposing the idea or distorting it so that it loses its identity.
- Search for different ways of doing things.
- Relax the rigid control of vertical thinking – perhaps by thinking in visual images rather than words.
- Make use of chance, be open to stimulus, make connections as in the example of Richard Feynmann and the spinning plate (see p. 136).

Learning to be creative

Creativity is not only an outcome of a good education, but a means of achieving a good education.

Professor Michael Barber, Standards and Effectiveness Unit, DfEE

As well as being creative in your learning, you can also learn to be more creative! Some traditional aspects of formal education may have stifled creativity but a dynamic approach to learning can help you to unlock your potential.

As well as being creative in your learning, you can also learn to be more creative!

Education and creativity

Tony Bates, in his book *Technology, Open Learning and Distance Education*, argues that we cannot justify a system of teaching – or training – which:

. . does not facilitate the vast majority of people to learn and think creatively and independently throughout their lives.

There is a view that education does not do enough to encourage and develop creativity – a highly structured curriculum, an emphasis on academic standards and other features of our present system embody a lot of the obstacles to creativity that we described earlier.

At present many educational systems favour those who produce technically correct, but not necessarily imaginative, work. We shall increasingly need people who do both.

Creative Teaching and Learning (Torrance and Ellis, 1971)

The more prescriptive the curriculum, the greater the need to be explicit about creativity and not leave it to chance.

Design Council

Creativity is not a simple matter of 'letting go' and we should not assume that creativity only emerges from free expression and a lack of inhibition or constraints. As we have seen in this chapter, creativity results from a range of intellectual processes, many of which are clearly focused.

People assume that as an innovator I break rules. I don't. I relish rules. I just like rewriting them.

Lord Stone of Blackheath

Creative education requires a balance between teaching knowledge and skills and innovation. Creative education is not a subject in the curriculum, it is a general function of education.

Setting out to embed the concepts of creativity deeply in the educational establishment is the greatest challenge, offering the greatest prize of all. That prize would be the realisation of an ethos of creativity, rather than a compartment of creativity.

Cape UK

All this means that organisations need to make an important investment in creativity. Here is one example:

Investing in creativity

The Peugeot-Citroën foundry near Moulins in France believe in encouraging staff to contribute ideas, and give them the tools to do so. They devote 4 per cent of the salary budget to training and have created a climate of quality and self-managing teams. Over two-thirds of all staff participate in their 'Programme for putting improvements and ideas into practice' which results in some 200 creative suggestions about the way work is organised every month.

Think widely to become more creative

- Identify your personal blocks or barriers to creativity and think about how you could overcome these.
- Set aside a time each day to let your thoughts flow freely.
- Use your intrinsic reasons for learning (see Chapter 2) to develop your creativity.
- Develop creative interests outside work – it will carry over into your job.
- Try to think of alternative solutions to all problems – big and small.
- Look for unusual connections, follow hunches.
- Keep a notebook or 'ideas file' and use it to record your creative ideas.
- Brainstorm individually and in a group at every opportunity.
- Get plenty of mental exercise through puzzles, games, etc.
- Use a different learning style – don't get stuck in a rut.
- Make use of other media – such as art, music or pictures.
- Develop a questioning attitude. Ask yourself why something is the way it is; ask yourself What if. . .?; as a customer think about how a service or product might be improved.

And this leads on neatly to the next chapter, which looks more closely at questioning and critical thinking.

Increasing your own creativity

Many of the other skills discussed in this book can help you to become more creative in your approach to learning. In particular, reflection and thinking about your own mental processes can enhance your creative activity and improve it. This self-monitoring, self-management and goal setting is at the heart of the demands of a future in which all of us will face new, complex, risky and changing situations. And creativity in learning encourages a sense of responsibility – it can help you to become a more independent and self-directed learner, as we shall see in Chapter 10.

You can improve your creativity in particular situations by using the techniques and ideas in this chapter. But if you really want to become more creative you will need to exercise your mind and get into the habit of thinking widely.

8 The questioning learner

Think it possible that you may be mistaken.

Quaker Faith and Practice (1995)

In this chapter we look at the implications than a dynamic and questioning approach to learning can have for the way that we go about our lives and our work. One of the most important implications is that someone who grasps opportunities to learn with both hands will ask questions – of themselves, of their colleagues and of the systems in which they work and live. And we acknowledge that there are some situations where there is a fine line to be drawn between a creative person who is constantly asking questions and someone who gets labelled a trouble maker.

We begin with a look at critical thinking. The aim of most degree courses is to encourage students to become critical thinkers – people who can ask informed and creative questions which help to advance their field of work. We look at some of the priorities involved in asking such questions and argue that this kind of questioning approach is needed in the workplace every bit as much as in the seminar room. And, whilst recognising that this approach may not be welcomed in every organisation, we examine how, within limits, it is both encouraged and required by organisations that have embraced the principles of total quality. The chapter explores:

- Thinking critically – the value of asking constructive and thought provoking questions in academic life and as a manager or a member of a profession.

- Can we trust the Internet? – how freer access to information puts even greater emphasis on the need for critical questioning.

- Questions for quality – parallels between contemporary trends in management and the concept of responsible freedom.

Thinking critically

... historically the questions that people have asked have turned out to be more important than the conclusions they reached.

George Kelly (quoted in Shotter, 1970)

An active approach to learning means that you will rarely be content to take things for granted.

An active approach to learning means that you will rarely be content to take things for granted. As you learn to reflect creatively on your own performance you will also question whether the time honoured ways of getting things done are necessarily the best ways. Could we get the job done more quickly, more cost effectively or to a higher standard? Questions like these will come naturally to a manager or professional who is ready to exploit the power of learning.

But this itself raises some important questions about our attitudes to learning, particularly at the organisational level. Quite frequently in our own work we are asked whether employers genuinely want people who are switched on to learning, who ask awkward or difficult questions. Surely they really want people who will get on with their job rather than rocking the boat? This provides the main theme of this chapter.

Our view is essentially positive. We are confident that more and more organisations *do* want people who ask unexpected questions – provided that they are informed, thoughtful and constructive. Provided, in other words, that the person raising the question has mastered the topic and mastered the art of asking constructive questions. And our view is that employers *need* people who are equipped to ask such questions. Until relatively recently, however, critical thinking has been valued more highly in academic circles than in the workplace. This is, in fact, one area where academic learning may have something to offer to management development.

Critical thinking at university

The focus of this book has been very much on learning at and for work. However we are conscious that you may be considering – or indeed working on – a more formal programme of learning such as an MBA or an advanced professional qualification. So to begin this chapter we will focus on the demands of a university level course, both to introduce the importance of critical questioning and to highlight the demands of a masters degree.

Developing a professional learning programme

A few years ago we were involved in the development of a professional learning programme which raised some interesting issues concerning the role of questioning in critical thinking. We are going to discuss this project at some length because it sheds light on the possible value of critical and creative questioning in the workplace.

The project concerned a national programme sponsored by the Department of Health in the UK. *Health PICKUP* is a scheme whereby healthcare professionals – mainly nurses but also physiotherapists, radiographers, occupational therapists and so on – can study a wide range of management topics such as budgeting, quality management, managing information, leadership and change management through programmes delivered at the workplace.

These programmes are supported by a series of specially developed workbooks and those who enrol also take part in a series of workshops facilitated by staff from their own hospital or general practice. The programmes are, in fact, highly practical. The workbooks are full of ideas for activities and each programme is rounded off by the participant carrying out a significant quality improvement project geared to their own organisation's real needs which they have conceived and executed themselves.

Gaining academic credit

Once Health PICKUP had been up and running for two or three years it faced its biggest challenge. A network of about 50 centres had been established and some real enthusiasm was building up. A major requirement emerged, however. Both participants and senior managers at the centres wanted those who had completed programmes to have the chance to gain formal credit for what they had learned.

Healthcare is a very interesting area in that, although learning provision at every level is primarily work based, 'academic credibility' is also highly prized. Vocational qualifications have never caught on amongst the established clinical professions. The recognised currency remains academic degrees or points towards academic degrees. The requirement was that the team responsible for Health PICKUP should make arrangements so that nationally recognised Credit Accumulation and Transfer (CATS) points could be awarded for each module, giving successful candidates something tangible to show for their work.

The CATS Scheme

The national Credit Accumulation and Transfer Scheme (CATS) has been operating since 1986. Originally set up by the Council for National Academic Awards (CNAA) it has the following aims:

- to widen access to higher education
- to enrich opportunities for continuing professional development
- to stimulate the use of employment-based learning for credit towards academic and professional awards.

Credit is available at four levels:

- Level 1 – equivalent to work during the first year of a degree course.

- Level 2 – equivalent to work during the second year of a degree course.
- Level 3 – equivalent to work during the final year of a degree course.
- Level M – equivalent to work towards a postgraduate certificate, diploma or masters degree.

The system is recognised and supported by every university in England and Wales.

Where no programme had gone before. . .

This was a demanding remit. The national agency responsible for the CATS scheme needed to be convinced that a programme delivered in the workplace and supported by clinical managers rather than university lecturers could meet their standards. And there were further complications. Members of the different professions involved in Health PICKUP would start their modules holding qualifications at different academic levels. Professions such as radiography, physiotherapy and so on are degree entry occupations: people with this background would be looking for credit at CATS level M. Most nurses, on the other hand, do not hold degrees: they would value credits at one of the undergraduate levels.

So, as the brief firmed up, it became clear that credit should be available for every module at each of the CATS levels. Candidates would be required to design projects which could be assessed at the relevant level, and clear criteria were needed so that they and the course tutors who would mark their work clearly understood what was required. Again this was a ground breaking development. No scheme with this level of flexibility had ever been submitted for CATS approval.

What are university degrees for?

This was where we become involved in the project. The CATS scheme had never published any guidelines on the standards of performance required at the different levels in the system. To a large extent it was comfortably assumed that university lecturers and examiners would 'know what they wanted when they saw it'. Now Health PICKUP would need to make these implicit 'taken for granted' assumptions explicit.

As a first step the team drew up a set of draft criteria which could be used in planning and assessing a work-based project against the CATS levels. To do this they paid attention to the results of a series of research projects into academic performance published by Elliot Jacques and his colleagues. Our task was to find out whether these research-based criteria matched up with those used day-to-day by staff in higher education.

We visited staff at three different universities. At two of them we met lecturers and course coordinators running nurse education programmes. At the third our contacts were in the department of visual arts, music and publishing. The aim was to show them the draft indicators and find out more about what they looked for in their students' work at different stages in their courses. In a real sense we were investigating the aims of university education – what were the skills and capabilities they were trying to encourage? The answers had a great deal to do with the ability to ask critical questions.

A very clear pattern emerged. As Jacques had predicted, there were qualitative differences between the standards set at each level. Students were not just expected to know more as they progressed through their courses. Rather they were expected to become increasingly sophisticated in the way that they *handled* this knowledge. In particular they were expected to move from a situation where they simply took in new concepts and findings to one where they could ask increasingly creative and incisive questions on the basis of this knowledge. The progression went like this (Figure 8.1):

░   At level 1 students are not expected to get involved in critical thinking at all. There is a great deal for them to find out; their priority is to get a good feel for the key concepts and techniques used in their chosen discipline.

░   At level 2 the student is still gaining knowledge but he or she is now expected to make comparisons between different areas or theories. The key words here are 'analysis' and 'synthesis' – the ability to bring two ideas together.

░   At level 3 – degree level – students are expected to go a stage further. In particular, they can find new ways of applying their knowledge

Figure 8.1 Four levels of academic performance

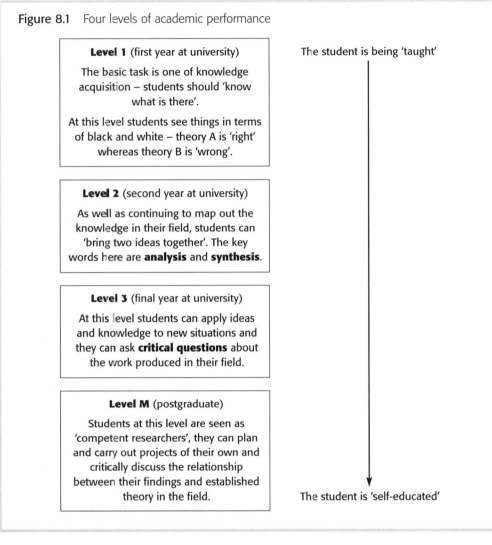

Level 1 (first year at university)

The basic task is one of knowledge acquisition – students should 'know what is there'.

At this level students see things in terms of black and white – theory A is 'right' whereas theory B is 'wrong'.

Level 2 (second year at university)

As well as continuing to map out the knowledge in their field, students can 'bring two ideas together'. The key words here are **analysis** and **synthesis**.

Level 3 (final year at university)

At this level students can apply ideas and knowledge to new situations and they can ask **critical questions** about the work produced in their field.

Level M (postgraduate)

Students at this level are seen as 'competent researchers', they can plan and carry out projects of their own and critically discuss the relationship between their findings and established theory in the field.

The student is being 'taught'

The student is 'self-educated'

and they should be able to ask critical questions about published papers and articles.

At level M asking critical questions becomes the routine task. Students at this level are researchers. They can ask totally new questions which will add to the knowledge available to their discipline and they can plan how they will answer these questions. For university education this represents the finished article. In a telling phrase, one lecturer described a successful student at this level as 'a flexible worker who can say what work needs to be done'.

As Figure 8.1 shows, there was another dimension to this. University students are expected to become increasingly independent as they move through the system. At the beginning they are very definitely being taught. Postgraduates, on the other hand, know their field well enough to have become much more independent learners.

To complete the story – we were able to make some revisions to the draft assessment indicators to bring them more closely in line with what the lecturers had told us. This was enough to convince the relevant committee that the Health PICKUP approach to credit rating was sufficiently rigorous to meet their requirements. Hundreds of professionals in the health service have now gained credits through this system.

Moving out of the lecture theatre

The important lesson that can be drawn from this work is that one of the main aims of university education is to help students learn to ask well considered but potentially provocative questions about their work, But for us the remarkable conclusion was that in the eyes of their lecturers even students who have completed a degree have only just begun to develop this capability. It is only at postgraduate level that the student is expected to be able to raise these questions in the way that a professional researcher would. So, with Health PICKUP it would only be the – relatively few – therapists aiming for level M credit who would be expected to ask searching questions about the management practices in their ward or department. Crucially, the many nurses who would be designing projects at level 2 would not be expected to ask any original questions or make creative suggestions – the guidance for planning a level 2 project actually suggests that simple data collection would be enough.

This was at odds with many of the changes that are taking place in the nursing profession. Increasingly, nurses are actively encouraged to question both managerial and clinical practice. Indeed, in the UK it is now a statutory requirement for nurses to 'blow the whistle' if they realise that a doctor – or any other professional – is acting incompetently and so threatening the health of a patient.

In academic circles the ability to ask critical questions is obviously seen as something that is restricted to a chosen few. There may be good reasons for this. There is all the difference in the world between a well informed question based on deep understanding of the underlying issues and an off-the-cuff remark made by an outsider. Degree subjects involve a wide range of information and a variety of concepts which can be used to structure this information. It may well take two or three years of study before an undergraduate has built up enough understanding to raise pertinent questions which are genuinely grounded in this body of knowledge. Indeed, the ability to ask such questions is one of the main ways of demonstrating this understanding.

Questioning working practices

In today's workplace, however, the capacity to ask critical questions cannot be restricted to a privileged elite. Here are some examples of the kinds of questions which crop up on a routine basis:

- A production manager in a tyre factory may question their health and safety record:
  Can we really afford to lose so many working days through avoidable injuries?

- A transport manager with a soft drinks firm might suggest persuading burger bars that they should be supplied with syrups that can be made up at point of sale:
  Should we really be spending so much money on ferrying water up and down the motorways?

- A farmer might question the environmental impact of their accepted procedures:
  Is it really cost effective to waste money spraying hedgerows as well as the crop itself?

Being in a position to ask questions like these depends on the power of learning in two ways:

- You need to have learned enough about the topic in hand to recognise its importance.

- You need to have learned how to put questions clearly and in a way which will invite a positive response.

Other chapters will have helped you to build up the required level of understanding. Here is our advice on how to frame critical questions in an appropriate way.

Asking questions that produce answers

There is a real art to knowing when, where and how to raise thought provoking questions. You need to check for yourself that the conditions are right. In the academic environment there is really only one condition that applies:

- You need to be sure that you really have absorbed and understood all of the relevant information and perspectives.

In a management or professional situation, however, you need to be comfortable that your question will provoke the right kind of response – that you are seen as someone who is helping to take your outfit forward rather than a wrecker or just an awkward customer. So two additional conditions apply:

- You need to be confident that the people who matter are ready to hear the question and respond to it. You may need to lay some foundations in advance.

- You also need to be clear that you are the right person in the organisation to raise the question. Is someone else better placed because of their situation or connections? If so, you may need to enlist allies in the right places.

It is important that you are aware of these conditions. As you become more creative in your approach to learning you will certainly find yourself asking critical questions more and more frequently. This is an inevitable consequence of your growing understanding of your work and situation.

Checklist – asking critical questions

This set of questions will help you to check that you are in a position to ask critical questions in a way which will provoke a positive response from your colleagues:

- Are you on top of the subject matter – do you really know and understand what you are talking about?
- Are your colleagues ready to hear what you have to say – or will it come as a bolt out of the blue?
- Are you putting the question to the right person or people?
- Are you the right person to ask the question?

Can we trust the Internet?

One area which puts the spotlight on the value of critical questioning is the Internet, and more particularly the World Wide Web. The Web is many things to many people, a diverse source of commercial opportunities, entertainment and information. In this sense it is a unique opportunity to learn about the latest developments. Some of the material on the web is amusing, some of it genuinely informative and, unfortunately, some of it is downright misleading.

Imagine that you are interested in a particular topic – say the latest research into renewable energy sources. You tap key words such as 'wind power' into a search engine such as AltaVista and within a few seconds you will be given a list of 20 sites which seem to be relevant to your topic – a good point to start browsing.

The material listed by the search engine will, however, be quite different from the contents page of an academic journal on the topic. When you visit your first four sites you might find:

- The home page of a company specialising in the development of wind turbines for power generation.

- A website posted by a local pressure group objecting to proposals to establish a wind farm at a well known beauty spot.

- The abstract of an academic paper reviewing a series of projects concerned with the economic viability of alternatives to fossil fuel.

- A website claiming to reveal details of a breakthrough in wind power which has in fact been posted as a hoax.

You may need all of your critical faculties to be able to weigh up the relative value of information offered by these different sources. You would certainly need to be alert to who has created each site and why.

Short-cutting the quality assurance process

In its present form the Internet is perhaps the ultimate expression of the concept of 'freedom of information'. Literally anybody with a credit card can post almost anything that they want. There is no censor– but there is also no referee or editor.

To understand the nature of the information offered by the Internet it is helpful to look at its origins. In many ways the Internet is the product of the information explosion rather than the mechanism which has created it. The impetus to establish the net came during the 1970s when researchers in many fields became frustrated with the long delays involved before papers appeared in print. The amount of research underway was burgeoning, more and more papers were being submitted, creating bottlenecks in the quality assurance process which had been developed over many years to make sure that critical questions were asked of the research before it saw the light of day.

Researchers looked to new technology as the solution to the problem and the Internet was born – initially as a way of sharing knowledge amongst a group of American universities. The bottleneck was removed because researchers were now able to share their findings directly before they had been refereed.

Cracking Fermat's last theorem

Simon Singh's best selling book *Fermat's Last Theorem* tells the story of how the English mathematician Andrew Wiles finally solved one of mathematics most long-standing problems. Fermat's last theorem, a conundrum closely related to Pythagoras' theorem about right-angled triangles, had attracted many of the most creative minds in mathematics over three centuries but remained unproven.

Wiles first announced his proof through a series of lectures given at an international conference in Cambridge in June 1993. Rumours had leaked out that something special was in store. The Internet buzzed with emails sent by those attending the conference back to their university departments. All over the world mathematicians used the Internet to keep in touch with Wiles' lectures as, over several days, they built to a dramatic climax. Inevitably, as the excitement grew the press got hold of the story. The day after Wiles' final lecture the 'breakthrough' appeared on the front pages of daily newspapers such as the *Guardian*, the *New York Times* and *le Monde*.

But although the world now knew about Wiles' solution, there was a delay of over a year before his actual paper appeared in print. There was a good reason for this. Wiles submitted his paper for publication virtually immediately. But once the proof, which ran to hundreds of pages, was available in black and white one of the academic referees found a potentially fatal flaw in Wiles' reasoning. Wiles was eventually able to re-work the solution to avoid the problem but it did involve a major rethink. And Wiles' concentration was not helped when, on 1 April 1994, a hoax email was circulated around the mathematical community claiming – quite fictitiously – that another researcher had been able to *dis*-prove Fermat's theorem!

The normal five-stage process illustrated in Figure 8.2 had become a two-stage process. This acceleration in the process of sharing information places demands on the learner because it short-cuts the quality assurance process. In the formal system the editor and referee are there to ask critical questions – and in fact only a minority of papers are immediately accepted for publication. Although readers will still ask critical

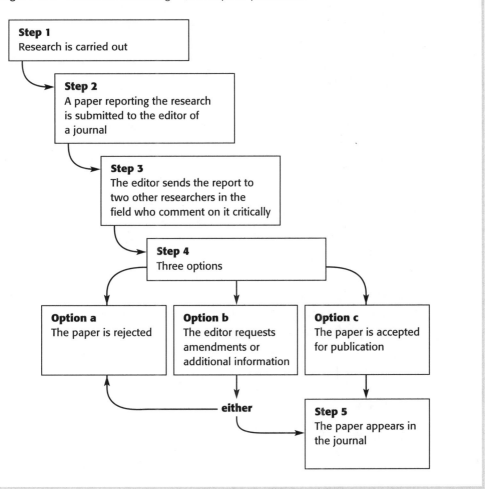

Figure 8.2   Academic refereeing – five steps to publication

questions about the paper, a number of key questions have already been put on his or her behalf. In the case of the World Wide Web you must usually ask these questions for yourself.

Ask more, and better, questions

You can use these guidelines for critical questioning whether you are reading text, using the Internet, considering a proposal, listening to others or solving a problem:

- Identify and challenge assumptions – where have they come from? Why are they accepted?
- Look for ambiguities – why do these exist?
- Be alert for lack of clarity – don't assume it's your fault if you don't understand something.
- Be wary of dogmatic statements – is the force of conviction more powerful than the argument supporting it?
- Explore alternative ways of thinking and acting, be open to new ideas.
- Try to spot contradictions in arguments.
- Check ideas out against your own experience – do they correspond with reality?
- Look for hidden bias or assumptions underlying ideas.
- Use the classic question words why, who, what, where, when and how? They are particularly useful for framing questions.
- Write your questions down to check that they are clear and coherent.
- Could someone misinterpret the question because of their own preconceptions or sensitivities?
- Ask the question to yourself – how does it feel? Does it appear aggressive or condescending?
- Avoid asking convoluted questions or more than one question at a time.
- Ask the question of the right person. Will they hear and understand the question you are asking?
- Reflect on the motive behind your question – is it genuine?
- Have you shied away from what you actually want to ask by asking a milder or more acceptable question?
- Make contact with like-minded people – questioning often involves risk taking and support from others can help.
- Remember – all problems can be turned into questions.

Questions for quality

Finally we must turn to one of the questions raised at the beginning of this chapter: Do employers really want people who ask critical questions?

We must admit that there is a great deal of force to this question. There are still plenty of managers and clients who seem to take their cue from Margaret Thatcher – who famously made it clear that she wanted

Do employers really want people who ask critical questions?

people around her who offered solutions rather than raising questions and problems. We met Chris Argyris' work on the 'defensive manager' in the previous chapter. Managers who fall into this trap stifle creativity and smother any attempt to raise critical questions about accepted practices. They do nothing to create a climate or environment in which active learning, which inevitably leads to new and unanticipated questions, can thrive. An appetite for learning could lead you into problems in organisations run along these lines.

There is a risk, however, of being too cynical in discussing this question. An increasing number of organisations do take positive steps to encourage a questioning attitude. The Coca-Cola Enterprises' SkillStart Programme is a good example (see Chapter 1). Here is a company which has made a sizeable investment in a learning programme designed to equip young people with the knowledge and skills necessary to ask critical questions about how work is organised and carried out. They very definitely do not want people who are mere machine minders. Rather, their aim is to help all of their staff to make a positive contribution to quality improvement, even if this does mean asking the occasional awkward question.

Quality management and responsible freedom

One of the most important factors working in favour of a more open and encouraging attitude towards questioning has been the quality movement. In many ways critical questions are the lifeblood of any quality system. Many of the features of quality management – from quality circles to suggestion boxes – are intended to provide a mechanism through which staff at every level can channel their critical questions in a constructive way. And, of course, quality management is often associated with a cultural change, one where the rewards and punishment are geared so that they encourage the right kinds of questions.

There are parallels here with Carl Roger's concept of 'responsible freedom'. A commitment to quality does not open the floodgates to continuous brainstorming. Rather, within certain limits, organisations are aiming for an atmosphere where staff feel free to ask questions in a responsible way – through the appropriate channels and with some thought given to likely reactions. An environment like this is much more likely to support active learning than the defensive climate Argyris found so frequently in his research. And it is also one where the spotlight is not just on the individual. TQM sees quality as a shared responsibility – a matter for teams and not just for individuals.

In this kind of set-up, learning is also unlikely to be exclusively a matter for individuals; compared with the academic situation, the workplace is likely to put greater emphasis on teamwork and the role of collaborative learning. This is the theme of our next chapter.

9 The collaborative learner

Earlier chapters have already hinted at the value of learning with other people – whether as part of a learning group, or by working with an individual coach or mentor who is not necessarily a professional educator but who can provide appropriate guidance and feedback.

This chapter looks at the value of collaboration in learning – and challenges the emphasis placed on competition through traditional education, training and assessment.

The chapter explores:

- Collaboration: strength in numbers – this section looks at the growing importance of groups and teams in work generally, and learning in particular.

- The power of group learning – this section describes a number of examples of collaborative learning.

- Learning in groups – this section looks at the skills you need to contribute to and manage group learning, in the process tackling some of the problems that can emerge during collaboration.

- Becoming a better coach? – this section looks at how managers and professionals can help other people to learn.

Collaboration: strength in numbers

There are three important reasons why collaborative learning is becoming more and more important:

- As a result of **changes in organisations**.

- As a result of **changes in education**.

- **The benefits of collaborative learning** are becoming increasingly obvious.

Changes in organisations

There has been a sea change in the way people work together in organisations over the last 20 years. Groups in general, and teams in particular, have become more and more important in successful organisations:

- Teams are central to managing quality. Quality improvement teams, quality circles and task forces have all been used to help organisations identify and tackle quality problems. Richard Schonberger, for example, argues that teams are crucial to world class organisations.

- Teams are seen as crucial to breaking down barriers between departments or sections. Multi-disciplinary teams bring together people from different parts of the organisation to pool ideas and to become more familiar with each other's ways of working. Rosabeth Moss Kanter argues that this is essential if organisations are to anticipate and manage change effectively.

- Even within departments or sections, there has been a move towards more collaborative working. The days when a manager could stand aloof from his or her team are long gone. Team working and leadership skills are now crucial to all managers.

These changes have given a major impetus towards more collaborative ways of working in general – and learning in particular.

Teams and total quality on a fruit farm

In one of our research projects I visited a 350-acre arable and fruit farm. The farm is staffed by a manager, foreman, two 'key workers', and casual staff at picking time. The manager has adopted a total quality approach rooted in a strong belief in the value of learning and teamwork. Continuous development is a priority for all staff – himself included.

The foreman has a key role to play in supporting learning; he works closely with the other staff and offers guidance, raises issues and answers questions. When key workers go on short courses at the local college, the foreman takes extra care to be on hand to help them apply what they learn.

The manager is convinced that this approach has paid dividends in terms of performance as well as making the farm a good place to work. He puts this success down to listening, talking and questioning in a context of fairness and honesty.

Changes in education

The changes in organisations parallel those in education. Traditionally, education included an important element of competition. Students were encouraged to work individually, and collaboration was often branded as 'cheating'.

Modern educational approaches are rather different. It is now much more common for students to work as groups, and indeed some assessment may be carried out as a group project.

Norm and criterion referenced assessment

An important factor underpinning the changes in education has been the trend from what is called 'norm referenced assessment' to 'criterion referenced assessment':

▓ If assessment is norm referenced, this means that the assessors expect a certain proportion of candidates to achieve specific grades, or to pass or fail. For example, the norm might be that 40 per cent will get Grade C, 20 per cent each will get Grades B and D, and 10 per cent each will get Grades A and E. Norm referencing encourages competition, as it is in each person's interest to try to do better than his or her fellow candidates.

▓ If assessment is criterion referenced, this means that each person is judged against a pre-set list of criteria. If 100 per cent of candidates meet the criteria for Grade A, they will all receive Grade A. Criterion referencing encourages collaborative learning, as it is in everyone's interest that the whole group does as well as possible.

In the past, much assessment was norm referenced. However, recent UK changes – in particular NVQs and GNVQs –have seen a trend towards criterion referencing.

The benefits of collaborative learning

Both these sets of developments stem from the growing realisation of the benefits of collaborative learning. Learning together means that:

▓ People can share their views, so ensuring a richer source and blend of ideas and experiences.

▓ People can share out roles and activities – for example, finding things out, doing some background reading or doing joint project work.

▓ People can support each other – giving feedback and encourage-ment, acting as a sounding board for ideas, reducing isolation.

Indeed, some people argue that collaboration is actually essential for learning. The ideas of the psychologist Vygotski, for example, contrast with the views of people like Skinner and Piaget who have focused on learning as an individual activity. For Vygotski (1978) 'human learning presupposes a specific social nature'. Much of our learning results directly from social interaction.

Collaborative learning across organisations

One project we work on involves collaboration across organisations. The Land-Based Colleges National Consortium (LBCNC) is a consortium of colleges in the land-based sector which work together with the following mission:

'Co-operation in the development and use of high quality flexible learning resources designed to encourage independent learning.'

A key aim of the consortium is to 'foster co-operation and collaboration between member colleges in the development and use of learning materials'. Examples of this collaboration include sharing resources, joint staff development and sector-specific discussion groups.

The power of group learning

Given the benefits of learning together, it is not surprising that a range of models for group learning have evolved. Here we describe some of the examples that we have worked with in recent years which seem to have been especially successful.

One project that John worked on shows the considerable potential for group learning.

Group learning in management development

The University of Cambridge Local Examinations Syndicate (UCLES, now OCR) is an organisation providing examinations and assessment within the UK and internationally. At the end of 1994 the organisation launched a management development programme designed both to raise levels of management competence and to encourage more independent learning. The programme was structured into a series of ten modules spread over a year, and participants had opportunities for NVQ assessment against the level 3 MCI standards.

The programme placed an important emphasis on collaborative learning. The group met together in monthly whole-day workshops, facilitated by a member of the internal development staff and a consultant. In between meetings they would take on a work-based assignment which asked them to reflect on a specific aspect of their work. The first half of each workshop was devoted to debriefing this assignment work while the afternoon sessions introduced the next topic.

The collaborative approach of the programme was popular with participants. One participant described how the programme 'has become an integral part of my job and has given me confidence' while another said that 'I'm gaining greater confidence (and ideas) of how to tackle my role and deal with my team'.

The time spent debriefing assignments proved particularly successful and the mornings became a forum for a free interchange of ideas and updates on work in progress. They provided an opportunity during which people could share feelings and experiences and a level of mutual trust developed. One person described the benefit of people:

'. . . telling me that what I have been doing is working and being given the encouragement to carry on trying to make changes.'

The approach led to important cross-departmental networking – as one participant put it:

'The programme provided a means of breaking down inter- and intra-departmental barriers.'

The approach also led to some exciting examples of people taking responsibility for their own learning. On some occasions, group members organised 'catch-up' sessions to brief people who missed a workshop. Towards the end of the programme the group took greater control of the afternoon sessions as well, to the point where they asked the facilitators to let them run things themselves. And participants continued to network and work together after the formal programme had ended.

Learning sets

The approach adopted by the management development programme owes much to the idea of 'learning sets' which originates from the action learning approach. Action learning operates according to a number of key principles, many of which reflect our own assumptions as highlighted in Chapter 1:

- That learning is effective if it is approached as an active process.

- That learners should be able to take charge of their own learning – including what, how and when they will learn.

- That groups provide a positive learning environment within which people can share ideas and support each other.

Learning sets are groups of learners who agree to work together. In the early stages at least they may be supported by expert facilitators who help to manage meetings and guide learning. However, in the longer term the groups will become self-managing – it is common, for example, for them to become the basis of longer term networking, as the following example shows.

Learning sets in workforce planning

In recent years there has been a growing recognition within the UK National Health Service that there is a clear need for effective workforce planning. Several factors have led to this need – the fact that staff make up 70 per cent of the cost of most NHS organisations, the changing and growing levels of patient need and problems with recruitment and retention of healthcare professionals.

During 1999 the NHS Executive for the South West commissioned Conrane Consulting, specialists in workforce planning and the health service, to work with a range of NHS Trusts across the South West of England to develop and apply a process for workforce planning.

The project established learning sets to bring together representatives from several organisations. The learning sets met together at approximately monthly intervals to work through the steps of the planning process in a cooperative and creative environment. They adopted an active, participant-led approach to learning and problem solving, supported by expert facilitators who were also able to provide coaching support between meetings. At key points during the project all the learning sets came together to share experiences and discuss progress.

The learning set approach proved both effective and enjoyable. As one participant commented, 'really enjoyable, we learned a lot from each other'. Northern Devon Healthcare Trust, one of the participating organisations, identified some important longer term trends and has been able to plan more effectively for the future – for example, looking at whether the acute or community sector should manage patient rehabilitation as stays in hospital become shorter. Wendy Brewer, a nurse manager with the Trust, felt she learnt a lot from taking part in the learning set – she has continued to work with people from the set as learning partners.

An extension of the learning set approach are self-help learning groups, where a group of people work together without a facilitator.

Learning partnerships

Groups are not the only way of learning collaboratively There is also scope for people to work in pairs, as in:

- Coaching and mentoring arrangements – where an experienced manager or professional commits to helping with someone's development.

- Learning partnerships – where pairs work together, for example joint pair work on projects or assignments.

The value of coaching and learning partnerships

Collaborative learning is central to the Coca-Cola/Enterprises' SkillStart Programme introduced in Chapter 1. Each SkillStarter is supported by his or her immediate team leader, who acts as a coach on day-to-day matters. In addition, each site has a mentor who works with all the SkillStarters on site and

who can provide support with other aspects of learning. The learning programme also encourages SkillStarters to work together in pairs or small groups
on assignments and projects. And it is not uncommon for new SkillStarters to
link up with an experienced SkillStarter who is further on in the programme.
There is little doubt that this level of support is central to the success of the
programme.

Virtual collaborative learning

Some exciting new examples of collaborative
learning are emerging from the Internet. The
scope that the Internet provides for people
to communicate quickly, cheaply and easily
over vast distances is helping break down
barriers to collaboration. It is particularly
relevant to the distance learning approach –

*Some exciting new
examples of collaborative
learning are emerging from
the Internet.*

distance learners have traditionally encountered major problems of
isolation and the Internet can help to reduce this, as the following
example shows.

Using the Internet in distance learning

The Institute of Education – part of the University of London – runs a distance
learning version of its MA in TESOL (Teaching English to Speakers of Other
Languages) which makes extensive use of the Internet. Students on the programme come from all over the country and, while they have an opportunity
to meet up for a weekend at the start of each module, otherwise work independently. The programme uses e-conferencing and email facilities to
promote group work among students:

■ Students work in groups of 12. Each fortnight a group works on a specific
task – which may be based around a video of a lecture from the face-to-
face version of the programme. Each student has their own individual task
and they circulate their work to other members of their group for comment
via the Internet. One person then brings together the work of the group.
Groups can also see – but not comment on – the work of other groups.

▨   In addition, a conferencing facility called 'the bar' gives students the chance to discuss a range of other, more general issues.

This facility has several benefits to the people taking part. It helps to overcome the isolation often experienced by distance learners. And it creates a real sense of group work – so important in professional and management development – that would not otherwise be possible.

Writing about her own experience of this course, Felicity O'Dell described some of the benefits she experienced:

'For me, the medium of the course has been at least as enjoyable as the message. It is fun being able to watch lecturers on video and while at times, one would like to be able to ask them a question or join in a discussion, there are advantages in being able to fit them in at five in the morning (or whatever suits your lifestyle), to put them on pause to make another cup of coffee or even, dare I say it, occasionally to fast forward.'

Learning in groups

Being able to learn collaboratively is, therefore, one of the crucial elements of the powerful learner. However, collaborative learning is not always successful – you have almost certainly experienced a group which worked badly and where you learnt little or nothing.

For collaborative learning to be a success, you need a number of important skills and I will discuss these shortly. However, underpinning these skills are some important attitudes and values, and these are central to establishing 'an effective human environment in which people can grow or develop' (Bentley, 1994). Two concepts from one of our learning gurus – Carl Rogers – are particularly relevant here:

▨   **Unconditional positive regard**. In *On Becoming a Person*, Rogers argued that within supportive relationships it is crucial to value and respect the personal worth of the other person or people. Collaborative learning is founded on just such an attitude. As a group member you should show positive attitudes towards, and respect for, your fellow learners. And if you facilitate a group then the relationship will work best if you demonstrate genuine confidence in individuals' abilities to make real progress in their professional development and to cope with and manage the stresses inherent in today's working environments.

Freedom with responsibility. In *Freedom to Learn for the 80s*, Rogers argued that people were best able to achieve their potential as learners in a climate of 'freedom with responsibility – a freedom in which the excitement of significant learning flourishes', where people are able to play an active and significant part in the learning process. This idea of responsible freedom is also crucial to the success of collaborative learning. On the one hand, collaborative learners need the freedom to experiment and to influence the style and content of their learning. At the same time, though, a relationship which offers freedom is open to deliberate or unconscious misuse – to make the most of collaborative learning you must use the freedom it offers responsibly.

Rogers went on to identify a number of qualities which in his experience were particularly likely to facilitate learning.

'Realness' or 'genuineness' – being able to convey an honest and open picture of yourself as a person.

Prizing, acceptance and trust – being able to accept and value the other person as a human being.

Empathetic understanding – seeking to understand the other person from their own perspective – to put yourself in their shoes.

So, if collaborative learning is to work, you need a positive climate of caring, openness, responsibility and trust, within which each individual applies a number of skills. We shall look at these next.

Group learning skills

Figure 9.1 shows those skills which an individual needs to possess in order to facilitate effective collaborative learning.

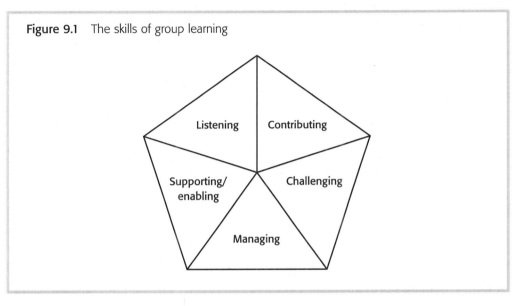

Figure 9.1   The skills of group learning

Listening

It is easy to think of listening as something passive. In practice, active listening skills are central to collaborative learning.

Contributing

One of the most important aspects of collaborative learning is the way that you and other members of the group make contributions to the discussion. Contributing to a group is not easy for everyone – you have to do a number of things at once: listening to what other people are saying; reflecting on what they say; marshalling your own thoughts; preparing what you want to say; and finding the right moment to intervene. Jean Ruddock describes how, by the time a nervous group member has put

Key skills in active listening

Focusing. Bring your mind to bear on what the other person is saying so you are not preoccupied with another issue or too busy thinking about what you will say yourself.

Using body language to show you are listening – for example, by maintaining regular eye-contact in a non-threatening way, and by sitting in a comfortable and relaxed way to encourage the other person to feel at ease.

Acknowledging. Nodding your head, using prompts like 'Uh-huh' and so on demonstrate listening and encourage the speaker to keep talking. Phrases like 'Ye-e-s', 'Go on' and 'Could you tell me a little more about this?' show the other person you are paying attention and invite them to carry on talking.

Drawing out the other person. Asking open questions can encourage the other person to say more. Repeating something they have just said encourages the speaker to say more without breaking their train of thought with a long question.

Checking understanding. Phrases such as 'It seems to me that you are saying. . .' or 'I get the idea that. . . ' let the other person know you are taking them seriously and gives you the chance to make sure that you are receiving the right message.

their thoughts together and done a silent rehearsal, the discussion may well have moved on and the contribution may no longer be apt. She also highlights that not everyone may feel comfortable with group learning; some individuals may not wish to become too involved.

At the other extreme, group members or indeed the facilitator can fall into the trap of monopolising too much of the discussion, preventing others from making a meaningful contribution of their own. In her book *Adults Learning* Jenny Rogers comments that some group members may even seize on the group as a chance to demonstrate how knowledgeable, insightful, quick-witted or sensitive they are, without really becoming engaged in the main work of the group.

Contributing effectively to a group therefore involves striking a balance between these two extremes.

Monitoring contributions

One way of monitoring contributions to a learning group is for one member of the group to keep a ticklist of who contributes. This involves listing the names of each group member and noting each time each person says something.

The group can then look at the levels of contribution made and discuss ways of changing how the group works.

Supporting and enabling

While contributing skills are clearly crucial to group learning, you also need to be able to support and enable other people. Ways of *supporting* other group members include:

- Looking for the strengths of the other people and the positive feelings you have for them.

- Keeping these strengths and positive feelings at the front of your mind during group sessions.

- Offering praise and encouragement when appropriate.

Ways of *enabling* other people to participate include:

- Actively inviting a contribution from someone who is not participating.

- Bring the discussion round to topics where you know they have ideas and experience.

- Expressing some of your own feelings and anxieties, and indeed mistakes you have made, so that other people feel better about expressing themselves.

- Showing other people that you care about their contributions – in particular by allowing them the time to express themselves.

- Suggesting that the group takes turns to comment on an issue.

If group members still find it hard to contribute, you can use techniques such as peer assessment and small group work.

Peer assessment as an enabling tool

Peer assessment is a valuable technique for enabling described by Heron. With a partner, you brainstorm the knowledge, skills, methods, attitudes and values that make for a high standard of work. Each person can then assess their own performance against these criteria for excellence, identify strengths and weaknesses, and invite feedback from the other person or people involved.

1   Select an area of work you are both involved in.

2   Together, brainstorm and list criteria for excellence in that area of work.

3   Individually, list three strengths and three weaknesses of your own performance in this area.

4   Share your self-assessment with the other person.

5   Invite feedback and suggestions for improvement from the other person.

Repeat stages 4 and 5, with the other person sharing their self-assessment and inviting feedback.

6   Create an action plan for how you can improve your performance in this area of work.

Challenging

The skills of supporting and enabling are the ones you will use most in collaborative learning. However, there may be times when you need to challenge people about their behaviour, attitudes and values – for example:

- If someone consistently fails to play their full role in the group.

- If someone regularly behaves inappropriately towards another member of the group – perhaps by putting them down or interrupting frequently.

- If it becomes clear that someone is not working to the appropriate professional or organisational standards.

> If there are differences of opinion between people in the group, you may need to find ways to allow people to express disagreement in a constructive manner.

If this happens, you may need to challenge the other person. To do this you need to be able to give feedback in a constructive way. One of our learning gurus, B. F. Skinner has written extensively on positive reinforcement or feedback and the following advice is influenced by some of his ideas.

Giving positive reinforcement

Feedback, which in Skinner's terms can be seen as an important form of positive reinforcement, is likely to be more effective if:

- **You focus on the behaviour rather than the person** – highlight what they did – 'I found what you said hurtful' – rather than personalising the issue – 'you're a difficult person'.

- **You describe the behaviour rather than judging it** – as in 'I felt you were quite aggressive towards Dave when we discussed. . . ' rather than 'what you did was awful'.

- **You give specific examples** – such as 'you interrupted Claire three times in succession' rather than 'you are always interrupting people'.

- **You listen to their point of view** – it is important to invite the other person to explain their behaviour so that you have more chance of finding common ground.

- **You look beneath the surface** – bear in mind that the behaviour could result from problems in the person's private life or elsewhere.

- **You look for alternative ways forward** – looking together for alternative solutions is more likely to be effective than telling someone what to do.

- **You own your feedback** – it's fine to say 'I think' or 'I felt'.

Managing a group

We have deliberately avoided making an artificial distinction between the skills of 'belonging to' and 'leading' a group. In our opinion, the powerful learner needs to possess the full range of collaborative skills, whether or not they formally lead a learning group. However, if you do become responsible for facilitating a learning group session, you will also need to manage group sessions.

Acting as a facilitator

The facilitator has a number of responsibilities. He or she will need to seek group agreement on:

- Practical issues such as when and where you will meet. The physical shape of the group – where and how they sit and so on – can have a very significant influence on how people behave.
- How large the group should be. Jean Ruddock suggests that 6–10 is about right, while Jenny Rogers suggests that 8–12 is appropriate.
- Ground rules: for example, about the kinds of issue that are appropriate for discussion, levels of participation or confidentiality.
- Agenda setting: what you will seek to achieve in the group session, which topics you will cover and how long you will spend on each.
- Timekeeping: how you will manage time so that you cover everything you wish to achieve – and what you will do if an issue seems likely to require more time than you have.
- Whether you will split into smaller groups.

Roles of a facilitator

Jean Ruddock describes a number of roles that a facilitator can play, each of which may be appropriate in different contexts or indeed at different times during a group session:

- The 'instructor' who takes a firm lead in the discussion.

- The 'chair' who concentrates on managing the discussion, seeking agreement and moving through the agenda.

- The 'participant' who joins in the discussion rather than seeking to lead it.

- The 'model' who tries to set an example by their own behaviour.

- The 'devil's advocate' who deliberately seeks to provoke discussion and debate by putting alternative views.

- The 'consultant' who only participates when the group asks him or her a specific question.

Splitting up a group

Many people feel more comfortable participating in a smaller group, especially in the early days until they become more comfortable expressing themselves. In addition, small group work can give people more opportunity to talk about their own problems and issues.

Options for splitting up a group

- **Working in pairs.** The group splits into pairs. Within each pair, one person introduces a critical incident or important issue from their own work. The person explains their own views and feelings about the issue, and then invites feedback and support from the other person. They then swap roles, and the second person explains an issue which they then discuss.

- **Working in triads.** A variation is for the group to split into threes. With this option, two people work as a pair while the third acts as an observer whose role is to reflect on and give feedback about how they work with each other.

- **Working in small groups.** Alternatively, you can split up into two groups of three or four people. In each group one person describes an incident or issue, and invites support and feedback from the others. With this model there may not be time for everyone to describe an issue each time; however, it should still give important scope for people to participate.

Figure 9.2 shows how a group session may then work.

Figure 9.2   Model for splitting up a group

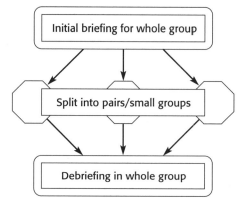

Becoming a better coach

So far this chapter has concentrated on the skills of group learning. However, it is equally important to consider the skills involved in one-to-one learning – and in particular the increasingly important context of coaching and mentoring. As a manager or professional – and especially one who has become a committed and powerful learner – it is very likely that you will be able to make a positive contribution as a coach or mentor.

■   **Coaching** – where a line manager or experienced professional is responsible for helping individuals or teams to learn. This is one of the most powerful methods available for helping people to learn. Bob Garratt describing companies who had experience of coaching, argues:

I believe that this is the most powerful and cost-effective of all the development methods. . . the benefits were immense as people took more responsibility for their work volume and quality.

Creating a Learning Organisation (Garratt, 1990)

░ **Mentoring** has much in common with coaching, except that a mentor is usually someone more senior – not necessarily the line manager – who takes an active role in helping someone's individual development and advocating them within the wider organisation.

The skills of group learning will clearly be crucial to this role as well. You will need to be able to listen, to support and enable and, on occasion, to challenge the person you work with. But there are in addition a number of other characteristics that mark out the good coach or mentor.

Above all, a coach is someone who can bring out the very best in another person and challenge them to achieve more than they might have felt possible. Garratt describes a coach as someone who sets mutually

░ Key coaching skills

In 1996 we carried out a review of the introduction of modern apprenticeships in a range of industries, published as *Learning by Design*. We found that people identified a number of characteristics of good coaches that were relevant across different occupations and organisations:

░ setting a clear example

░ explaining how to do things and why things should be done in a certain way

░ encouraging people to take responsibility and make decisions

░ identifying tasks that will challenge people

░ agreeing realistic targets

░ asking people questions about their work

░ listening carefully to what people have to say

░ giving constructive feedback – and praise – whenever it is due

░ making time for people.

agreed targets with individuals and teams, plans how to achieve them, delegates the authority to achieve them, and then lets them get on with things while providing appropriate support and monitoring. But, as Tom Peters and Nancy Austin put it, coaching is not about memorising techniques:

It is about paying attention to people – really believing them, really caring about them, really involving them.

A Passion for Excellence (Peters and Austin, 1985)

A coach in action

When John began work his first manager, Tony Bates, was an excellent coach. Tony's strengths included:

- His remarkable level of belief in me and my abilities (which seemed to me at the time completely unfounded!).
- The fact he was always available to help with problems and queries.
- The way he helped me think through and solve problems.
- The fact that while he would always offer constructive feedback on my work, he supported me fully when talking to other people.
- The general support and encouragement he gave.

Important as collaborative learning is, there will be times when you need to work alone. The next chapter goes on to explore the growing importance of independent learning.

10 The independent learner

The pace of life and demands placed on managers and professionals often means that many cannot afford the time to attend a full-time course. This has led to a growth in more flexible provision designed to overcome such difficulties. You may know this as open learning, distance learning, independent study or flexible learning – the sort of courses where the emphasis is on independent, self-managed learning as opposed to teacher or trainer-directed study.

Over the past 25 years the delivery of courses and programmes through open and distance learning has become a major growth area. The number of companies using open learning for employee development, coupled with the use of open learning in colleges and universities, has greatly expanded its use in education and training.

A review of recent thinking in lifelong learning (DfEE, 1998) talks about how the 'globalisation of the learning market' will require more open learning 'in order to establish an extensive infrastructure of learning opportunities in the home, the community and the workplace'.

This chapter explores issues in independent and open learning, and in particular:

- Going it alone?

- What is open learning?

- What makes for good learning materials?

- Independence not isolation.

Going it alone?

All learners are independent to some extent. No one can learn for you, and in any formal programme there will always be tasks that you have to tackle for yourself: reading, practising, writing assignments and so on. But many managers and professionals opt for an open or distance learning programme in preference to a taught course at a college or university. Here are some examples:

- A building society manager learning about new structures and services from company-specific learning material.

- An HR manager preparing for the IPD qualifications through a university.

- A graduate training as a Certified Accountant through the specialist open learning programme offered by the Chartered Association for Certified Accountants (ACCA).

- A teacher studying for a Masters in Education with the Open University.

Why do they do it?

This chapter draws heavily on a research project that Anna carried out in which she investigated learners' own views and experiences of their open learning programmes. One of the first questions she asked in her interviews was 'Why have you chosen open learning as a method of study?' As one might have expected, their answers stressed the importance of flexibility. They said that being able to study at a time, place or pace which suited them was an important or essential factor in their decision.

These open learners needed to fit their study time around work or family commitments. But, unpacking this a little more, the crucial factor was usually time:

I work full time and there are restrictions on study leave.

It's flexible – I can manage study around my complex time.

I can take the distance learning with me and do it on the train on the way to and from work.

I can learn at home, at my own pace and it fits in with work.

So one of the main reasons that you might opt for this kind of learning programme yourself at some point could well be that it fits in with your life and career priorities as a whole. But it is worth recognising that you may actually prefer to study this way, like the people who made the following comments:

If I don't understand something I can put it down and come back to it.

There's no immediate peer pressure – if you haven't understood something, you can quietly go back whereas in a group situation you fall behind

This chapter will help you to make a considered decision on whether the open learning option is for you. And it will also help you to get the most out of any such programme, helping you to know what to look for in choosing materials and gaining help and support when you need it.

It is also possible that in your role as a manager you may need to consider whether your organisation could make more use of open learning methods. Again, this chapter should help you to appreciate the issues involved and to make an informed contribution to the debate.

What is open learning?

Open learning is now an accepted part of the professional development scene but it is an area that remains slightly controversial. Is there really any difference between open learning and plain, old-fashioned correspondence courses? And can an open learning programme ever be as 'good' as a taught course? Those involved in developing open learning courses – and this is one of the main ways that we, the authors of this book, earn our living – in fact claim that this approach offers some real advantages over more traditional methods.

Breaking down barriers

The phrase 'open learning' is probably best seen as an umbrella term which covers quite a wide range of different types of provision including distance learning, flexible learning, correspondence courses, home study, resource-based learning and supported self-study. At heart, all of these have their origins in correspondence courses – which have actually been around for a long time. Pitman offered correspondence courses in secretarial skills in 1840, and distance courses in accountancy have been available since the early 1900s.

The basic idea behind all of these programmes has always been to make learning 'more open' by removing some of the unnecessary barriers which can limit access to taught courses. But, as the following quote from Roger Lewis and Doug Spencer shows, the introduction of the term open learning is meant to imply that this independent approach need not be second best; in some circumstances it may offer advantages that go beyond simply fitting in with your other commitments. Lewis and Spencer define open learning as:

. . . . a term used to describe courses flexibly designed to meet individual requirements. It is often applied to provision which tries to remove barriers that prevent attendance at more traditional courses, but it also suggests a learner-centred philosophy.

What is Open Learning (Lewis and Spencer, 1985)

Focusing on the individual learner

So open learning is no longer restricted to isolated individuals who live miles away from their nearest college or university. Instead, it is also justified in that it offers greater freedom and autonomy in learning. In the best examples, the people who have planned these programmes have made a genuine attempt to take account of how people really learn. John Coffey provides a particularly clear explanation:

An open learning system is one in which the restrictions placed on students are under constant review and removed wherever possible. It incorporates the widest range of teaching strategies, in particular those using independent and individualised learning.

'Open Learning Opportunities for Mature Adults' (Coffey, 1977)

Features of open learning

We can get a clearer picture of what an open learning programme looks like in practice from the following list of features given by Derek Rowntree in his book *Preparing Materials for Open, Distance and Flexible Learning*. He argues that learning in this way involves you in:

- taking responsibility for your own learning
- learning alone or in small groups
- learning at your own pace and time
- learning from text materials and other media
- learning actively, rather than passively
- learning with less frequent help from a teacher.

So, compared to a conventional course, materials carry more of the weight with relatively little or no reliance on direct teaching.

The theories behind open learning

Open and distance learning is based on some important underlying theories of learning, many of which you will encounter elsewhere in this book.

Skinner (1953)

Skinner's emphasis on the role of positive reinforcement is integral to open learning, both in materials and through the role of the tutor.

Bloom (1956)

Explicit learning objectives are a prominent feature of most open learning materials. Bloom's taxonomy of learning objectives has had a strong influence on this aspect of open learning.

Gagné (1965)

Robert Gagne's work on the organisation and structure of learning has had a major impact on the way in which open learning materials are written and presented.

Freire (1972)

Two aspects of Freire's work are central to the philosophy of open learning: the concept of inclusion and the principle of creating a dialogue with the learner.

Rogers (1983)

Carl Rogers is best known for his work in the development of client-centred counselling but he also originated the idea of student-centred learning – a key principle in open learning.

How 'open' does learning need to be?

Although most programmes share the features highlighted by Rowntree, not all open learning provision follows the same pattern – and in any case all learning programmes, even taught courses, involve some element of openness. Lewis and Spencer made this point by introducing what they called the 'open learning continuum'. They suggested that we should look at a number of 'dimensions' of openness such as start dates, time and place of study (see Figure 10.1).

We must point out that 'more open' is not necessarily better. Indeed there may be some very good, learner-centred reasons for making some aspects of a programme less open: a completely open course could lack focus and structure and simply lead to confusion. Carl Rogers' idea of responsible freedom implies a certain amount of structure. We all need some boundaries – deadlines for assignments, recommended reading lists and so on – so that we know the limits to our freedom.

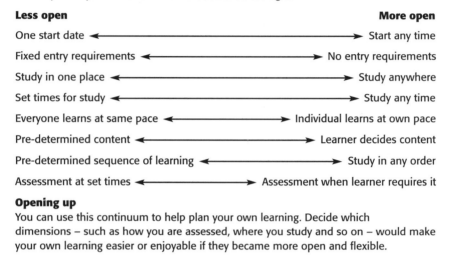

Figure 10.1 Dimensions of openness

Below are some of the dimensions in which learning can be opened up, each becomes more open as you move towards the column on the right.

Less open   **More open**

One start date ⟵⟶ Start any time

Fixed entry requirements ⟵⟶ No entry requirements

Study in one place ⟵⟶ Study anywhere

Set times for study ⟵⟶ Study any time

Everyone learns at same pace ⟵⟶ Individual learns at own pace

Pre-determined content ⟵⟶ Learner decides content

Pre-determined sequence of learning ⟵⟶ Study in any order

Assessment at set times ⟵⟶ Assessment when learner requires it

Opening up
You can use this continuum to help plan your own learning. Decide which dimensions – such as how you are assessed, where you study and so on – would make your own learning easier or enjoyable if they became more open and flexible.

The growth of open learning

So far we have concentrated on open learning mainly from the point of view of empowerment and enjoyment: it can be liberating and satisfying to learn this way. But the growth of open learning has also been stimulated by economic considerations.

Government initiatives. . .

The UK is generally recognised as a leader in the field of open learning. A great deal of the impetus for this has come from government initiatives like the Open University, which were intended to increase the number of people who had access to higher education. The new University for Industry (UfI), announced by the Labour government almost as soon as it came into power, is merely the most recent example of developments intended to increase the nation's competitiveness.

Key dates in the development of open learning in the UK are as follows:

- **1965** – The National Extension College (NEC) was set up as a charitable trust to give home-based adults a 'second chance' at academic or vocational studies using correspondence materials, broadcast television and support from local tutors.

- **1971** – The Open University (OU), the world's first university to teach at a distance, admitted more than 24 000 students in its first year. It pioneered admission without qualification and modular courses. Its undergraduate programme is still the main activity but continuing education, such as The Open Business school, is expanding fast.

- **1983** – The Open Tech Programme was not an institution, but an initiative. The then Manpower Services Commission spent £45 million on 140 projects intended to develop, deliver and support open learning in vocational training.

- **1987** – The Open College was established to transform vocational education and training much as the OU had transformed higher education. It received £100 million funding but failed in the requirements to become self-financing and folded in 1996.

- **1997** – The University for Industry (UfI) was established. The UfI aims to make extensive use of new technology to provide a national training structure which can be used in industry, higher education and by individuals to improve their occupational knowledge and skills.

In addition, there are numerous government programmes, both in the UK and through the European Union, which fund projects designed to develop and promote open learning approaches.

. . . and company initiatives

Open learning is also increasingly used by commercial companies as a means to develop their own employees; examples include the Rover Group, the Post Office, and the banking and retail industries. A recent survey (Department of Employment, 1993) revealed that open learning was used by 34 per cent of large employers. And, partly stimulated by the pressures of expansions and the need to generate revenue, many universities and colleges have also begun to offer open programmes.

Three components of open learning

For an open learning system to be successful it must have three key components. These are an effective management system, learning materials and learner support (see Figure 10.2).

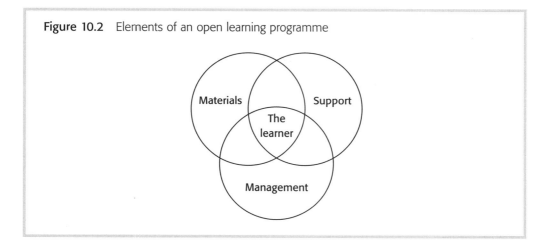

Figure 10.2   Elements of an open learning programme

While a clear management system is needed for activities such as supporting staff, keeping records, managing budgets, resources and facilities and evaluating and monitoring provision, in the rest of this chapter we shall focus on the other components of open learning that may have the most impact on you as an independent learner: materials and support.

What makes for good learning materials?

A major component of most open learning provision is the use of specially prepared or adapted learning materials:

The freedoms of open learning, such as those of time, place and pace, are usually made possible by giving the learner a package specially designed to enable him to learn on his or her own for at least some of the time.

What is Open Learning (Lewis and Spencer, 1985)

Learning material might take the form of:

- workbooks
- audio tapes
- videos
- CDs
- on-line resources
- textbooks/readers.

What to look for in materials

Like teaching, the quality of open learning materials can be immensely variable. Materials are a vital component of any open learning programme; they need to be of the highest quality to be effective. This need not mean they must be expensively produced – just as a flashily presented package may be a dismal failure because of poor learning design, so a cheaply reproduced workbook which has been well put together can prove highly successful, given the right management and support systems.

Materials are a vital component of any open learning programme; they need to be of the highest quality to be effective.

So what represents quality in open learning materials? One starting point is to say that many of the qualities which mark out an effective teacher also hold good for effective learning materials.

Characteristics of effective teaching – and effective materials

A good teacher and effective material:

- gives a clear explanation of the content of a programme of study
- gives clear objectives
- asks questions and provides opportunities for activity and participation
- gives the chance to practise skills and rehearse knowledge
- provides feedback and comments on performance
- gives hints on how to tackle tasks
- explains difficult ideas
- breaks learning into manageable chunks
- communicates clearly and appropriately
- highlights key points
- provides variety
- listens to criticism and feedback
- establishes a positive relationship.

Surprisingly, however, there has been relatively little investigation of how learners actually judge the quality of the materials they use. Anna looked at this issue in the research for her master's degree. She compared the ideas on the features of effective packages highlighted in a number of the guides produced by 'experts' in the field with those stressed by a sample of managers and professionals who were studying open learning programmes. She found some interesting similarities and differences. The picture as a whole could help you to choose between the various packages that are on the market.

What do the experts say about learning materials?

A number of experts have produced guidance on writing open learning materials. Derek Rowntree, a professor at the OU, is one of the best known names in the UK open learning arena. In his latest guide, Derek Rowntree argues that open and distance learning materials should be:

... put together in such a way that users can learn from them satisfactorily with less help than usual from a teacher.

Preparing Materials for Open, Distance and Flexible Learning (Rowntree, 1994)

Rowntree informs us that objectives play a big part in open learning since they tell learners what they might get out of the material, and he emphasises the importance of activities in stimulating active learning.

An appropriate style

Rowntree also argues that materials need to be 'reader friendly' which means being conversational, welcoming, and 'speaking plainly', following the plain English principles of short familiar words, using the active tense and ensuring that sentences and paragraphs are short. Janet Jenkins offers three guidelines for writing simply:

Be clear about what you want to say,
say it clearly and simply in an appropriate style
and test what you have written to see if people can understand.

Materials for Learning – How to teach adults at a distance (Jenkins, 1981)

An interactive approach

Roger Lewis, formerly BP Professor of Open Learning at the University of Humberside, is a prolific author of open learning texts and writes widely on the subject. Writing with Nigel Paine he tells us that what is 'special' about open learning is arousing interest, objectives, structuring content, giving practice, attending to the difficult and creating 'two-way communication'. They suggest that:

... the text itself should include the interactive features at the heart of open learning: self assessment questions, activities and other means.

How to Communicate with the Learner (Lewis and Paine, 1985)

A clear structure and signposting

Lewis and Paine give particular attention to structuring and signposting a package by 'chunking' – breaking material into manageable pieces. They recommend that each chunk or segment should have a title, content, objectives, prerequisites or diagnostic test and time indications. This emphasis on chunking and sequencing is echoed by Sims who states that:

The course materials are prepared to make what is to be learned as clear as possible, to arrange and present the subject in small, easy to master, steps.

The Search for Purpose in Correspondence Education (Sims, 1996)

The right workload

Lewis and Paine also stress the importance of setting a realistic workload, warning that materials can take longer to master than the writer intended with the result that 'learners often turn off because they cannot cope with the great bulk of the package'.

Ellie Chambers looks at ways of assessing learner workload, asserting that:

The amount of work learners are expected to do crucially affects their attitudes to distance and open learning courses and their ability to complete them successfully.

'Assessing Learner Workload' (Chambers, 1994)

She argues that, if a course is overloaded, learners will need to make selections from the curriculum, even if they have little prior knowledge of the subject on which to base their decisions. Alternatively, they will simply drop out. Woodlett and Parlett (1983) found that with Open University students there was a general tendency for dropout rates to increase with workload.

Using different media

The experts also stress the value of using a range of media. The Open University has made extensive use of radio, television and audio and video tapes. Radio has been used to deliver open learning in programmes across the world, many packages contain audio cassettes and, more recently, computers and the Internet have been used both to deliver learning and to provide support.

However, it is clearly crucial that media are used in appropriate ways, and not just to provide unnecessary glitz. Tony Bates, a leading expert on broadcasting and technology in open learning, argues that 'the appropriate choice and use of technologies will depend on the particular context in which they are used'. He stresses that a number of factors should be considered when selecting media, including access, cost and the kind of learning involved.

This suggests that the current fashion for using computers and the Internet in open learning must be considered critically. Clearly – as we saw in Chapter 9 – they can provide invaluable aids to learners. However, if presenting materials on computer increases both the cost and the inconvenience to the learner, it is time to rethink!

The 'expert' view: a synthesis

A synthesis of the main points from the experts suggests that open learning materials should have the following features:

- objectives
- activities – to aid active learning
- feedback
- written in clear language
- a friendly, personal style
- a clear structure
- material broken into 'chunks' or steps
- a realistic workload
- a sense of dialogue through two-way communication
- graphic elements.

And what do learners think?

Anna's interviews with open learners confirmed many of the features of quality materials identified by the experts. But there were some important differences. And learners are more willing to prioritise. They clearly thought that two of the features – writing style and a clear, logical structure – were much more important than the others. And there were some surprises. Two of the features of open learning material regarded as absolutely crucial by all open learning authors – clearly stated objectives and interactive activities – were less highly prized by the learners themselves.

Writing style

Learners gave a clear indication that they respond positively to material which is written in a straightforward style and which is interesting and involving. They prefer it to be written as a dialogue with an adult and they shun anything which seems patronising. Favourable comments were:

Well worded.

Basic language.

Plain English.

Direct and to the point.

Adult language. Not patronising.

Little room for misunderstanding.

There was no pomposity, it was erudite but understandable. The style accommodated the learner's position.

Written so that the writer is talking to you. A dialogue as opposed to a monologue.

Learners did not like materials which they described as:

Dry.

Some wording was difficult.

The way it is written is too complex and dense. There are too many unusual words. There's far too much academic language. The guy who wrote it likes to find the most obscure word rather than plain English.

Logical structure and sequence

Anna's research confirmed the importance of logical structure and sequencing. Learners made the following points:

Followed the learning cycle.

Well structured.

They'd obviously thought about the order and the relationship between things.

Bite-sized chunks.

It was in blocks. A nice pattern of assembling knowledge, further thought and con-clusions – really well designed and thought through. It was the first time I've come across learning materials that did that for me.

Good signposting and referencing.

Easy to find things when referring back.

Anna's interviews also pointed to referencing and cross-referencing as important criteria. Learners wanted to be able to identify easily relevant sections for assignments and revision.

Presentation of objectives

Objectives, which are considered essential in all the literature on writing open or distance learning material, are not considered particularly important by learners. Perhaps these are more significant for writers because of their function in checking that their material delivers the intended learning – it may not follow that they need to be reproduced in the actual learning material.

Activities and feedback

There is little evidence that activities – a key component of open and dis-tance learning – are seen as an important feature by all learners. Most of the people Anna talked to skipped some or most of the activities in their packages. Where it was suggested how much time to take over an activ-ity, participants reported that they nearly always spent less time than was recommended.

It is important not to overstate the position. These learners were not calling for activities to be dropped from their programmes. Indeed, less than a fifth of those interviewed thought that there were too many activities in their materials and there were a number of positive comments:

The level varies – and that's good.
They stimulate the right kind of question.
The best activities are real and relevant.

There were however a number of adverse comments about the quality of specific activities, particularly ones which seemed simplistic, obvious or irrelevant:

Sometimes the answer seemed obvious – you think you've got it wrong because it's too easy.
There are far too many as far as I was concerned because I consider them a waste of time – I happily skip them.
I'd like to know how much they want. I'd rather be told how many words rather than time. They gave you a time they allowed – say 20 minutes. If I do it in 10 minutes, I think I must have left something out.
They are offensive and irrelevant.

Perhaps the lesson to be drawn is that authors are wrong to think that people necessarily have to write answers to activities to add interest and involvement to the text. When you look at open learning materials you should check not just for how many activities have been included but whether these activities genuinely add learning value.

On the other hand, feedback to activities was viewed very positively and was generally described as helpful and relevant. Feedback to activities contributes to the creation of a dialogue, and this was one of the main reasons why learners valued it.

Positive comments included:

Helps me to know where I'm getting it wrong.
I would tend to worry that I'm not doing it right (the feedback) puts your mind at ease.
Reinforced and made you think of things you hadn't considered.

Helps you to know what points you should have included.

I do my activity before I read their ideas so it's interesting comparing. I normally find I've got close to 60 per cent of their points so I get another four – which is useful.

Learners did not find feedback helpful if it was too vague or where it failed to explain their errors.

Design for learning

A clear finding which emerged was that learners recognise and value graphic design and page layout which help them to understand and use materials. While learners also react favourably to material which uses colour and illustrations and has a smart, glossy cover, the interviewees who were using less expensively presented material did not criticise the lack of these features. Conversely, participants criticised layout which was 'dense', without enough sub-headings or which resulted in them 'getting lost'.

So the most important design features are those that promote learning and understanding. Participants said that this is helped by wide margins which give space for notes, clear print size, use of headings, creating blocks of text and using a particular style for different types of material such as case studies or activities.

Perhaps this is best summed up by the interviewee who described the design of her package as:

Easy on the eye and the brain.

Clear and simple

The overriding message which emerges from these learners, most of whom were studying at higher levels or for professional awards, is the need for clarity. Clarity in writing, clarity in presenting and ordering information, clarity in the type of activity and feedback – all bound together by a clear design which helps learners move smoothly through the material.

Quality check – materials

This checklist is based on the factors which experienced open learners say make for quality materials. You can use it to review any package you might be considering using whether it be print based or in any other medium.

- Is text written in a clear and straightforward style?
- Does the tone of writing suggest an adult-to-adult dialogue?
- Is information presented in a logical order? – review a section and check that you can follow and understand it.
- Are sections an appropriate length? Are sub-headings regular and informative?
- Are activities relevant, interesting and varied?
- Will learners be able to answer activities accurately? Are any activities simplistic or pointless?
- Is feedback to activities direct rather than vague and does it explain where learners may have gone wrong?
- How easy would it be to review materials for assignments or revision?
- Is the design and layout spacious with clear print and good use of illustrations?
- Is technology and other media used to enhance the learning and not simply for 'glamour'?

Independence not isolation

Open learning, quite rightly, places importance on the principle of learners taking responsibility for, and managing, their own learning. Many of the terms used within open learning, such as self-study or self-managed learning, underline this philosophy.

In the early days of open learning there was a view, reinforced by many of the organisations trying to 'sell' the approach to employers and colleges, that it could provide a cheap alternative to training courses or lessons. One of the justifications for this claim was that the materials could replace training or teaching staff. Organisations which tried to do this found that their open learning initiatives failed: materials alone cannot sustain a quality open learning programme.

This demonstrates just how important the support function is. Frequently it is the quality and availability of support which is the determining factor in the success or otherwise of any open learning provision. No matter how good the materials are they will not work unless learners are provided with the right level of appropriate support.

Building a partnership

In practice a balance needs to be struck between encouraging autonomy in learning and providing the right level of support to ensure successful learning: it can be difficult to get this right. Open learners need sensitive, tailored support – people will not learn to take responsibility simply by being thrown in at the deep end!

Open learners need sensitive, tailored support.

The important thing for the learner and the supporter to determine is is how they will share the responsibility based on what the learner feels they need and what the supporter is able to offer. These responsibilities need to be made explicit – perhaps in writing.

Who are the supporters?

Open learning supporters often come from two backgrounds:

- **From education** – teachers and lecturers with experience of teaching and who are used to dealing with learners.

- **From industry** – managers and work-based coaches who may have little previous experience of training others in a formal sense but may have greater experience of individual coaching.

For each, this role represents both a challenge and an opportunity: an opportunity because it provides a chance to develop new skills; a challenge because it places new demands on people who are often already under pressure in their work.

Key stages in the support process

Drop out is often a problem in open learning – many learners do not complete their course of study. A great deal depends on the quality of the relationship built between learners and coach or tutor. Figure 10.3 illustrates three of the stages in the growth of such a relationship.

Figure 10.3 Stages in a supportive relationship

Getting started

Getting things off on the right footing is vital to future success. The open learning component may be part of a wider programme of learning which includes other forms of delivery. It is crucial that the open learning is placed in context, so that you can see how it fits into your overall course or programme. In education, this means making links with other parts of the course. In industry this may mean making links with the job or explaining how the learning relates to the overall aims of the organisation.

↓

Getting going

At this stage the supporter and learner need to draw up a plan for how the learning will be tackled. This may well involve selecting which parts of the material to use, negotiating and setting targets for completion, agreeing timescales and planning supporter/learner contact.

↓

Keeping going

Once the programme is underway it is up to the supporter to help maintain the pace, to provide detailed feedback, to monitor plans and ensure targets are met. Almost by definition, open learners have other demands on their time and other priorities.

Overall, these stages describe a developing relationship, one where the learner feels confident enough to become more independent and autonomous because they can trust the safety net offered by their coach or tutor. This relationship must be built with trust and care. Disappointingly, relatively few of the learners Anna interviewed for her research could say that they had experienced such a relationship. Even though they had access to support and were encouraged to contact their tutor or mentor the majority had never asked for help when they came up against a problem. Too many of them were worried that their tutor would think that they were stupid and that this might affect their assessment:

I didn't know the man, you feel stupid. He'll think I'm thick.

You feel you have to have a really 'worthwhile' question.

I would feel awkward phoning up a tutor and asking, 'What does this mean?'

I don't think I would have found it very comfortable to phone someone; I prefer face-to-face.

When it's the person who's going to be marking your work, you wonder how it will affect your results.

As a powerful learner it is important that you are ready to share the responsibility for the success of this relationship. You yourself have skills that can be brought to the table. Many of the qualities of collaborative learner considered in Chapter 9 are highly relevant and will help you to make sure that you receive the support you need as and when you need it.

Finding the right support

Anna's findings also revealed some unsatisfied support needs. Most of the learners would have liked more contact with others in the same position. Comments made about this form of support included:

I would have liked more group sessions and opportunities for discussion and debate.

I like talking to other students. Because it's more relaxed – you can explore ideas without feeling or sounding silly. I think it's a much easier way of learning than from tutors because you know the tutors know it and what they are expecting and what they want.

Some open learning programmes do include arrangements designed to bring learners together in this way – if not face-to-face then over the Internet – and this is likely to be an increasing trend. But if you do opt for an open learning programme at some point in your career you may like to think in advance about whether there are any friends, colleagues or relatives to whom you could turn for this kind of support.

Getting the right support

- What aspects of the learning do you think you will need most support with? For example, assignments, feedback, understanding the subject?
- What support is offered by the open learning provider?
- How can you access the support – phone, email, post, etc.?
- Will you be able to use the support at times which are convenient to you?
- Do you believe you have the confidence to use this support effectively?
- Are there opportunities to get in touch with other learners?
- Are there other people such as colleagues, friends or family who can give additional support?

This brings us to the end of a series of chapters which have focused on what it takes to become a powerful learner – the importance of becoming capable, reflecting on experience, using creativity, questioning things and being both collaborative and capable of working independently.

The last two chapters will take a broader view. In Chapter 11, we explore how the idea of 'career learning' gives some important pointers to the role of learning in the changing world of work.

11 Career learning

A lot of what we do is helping people to understand what their learning has been about.

Bill Davies – Careers consultant, Learning Partnership West

This chapter looks at how you can take an active, questioning approach to learning at every point in your working life. We revisit the idea of the 'learning lifeline', stressing that our learning priorities may vary at different times in our lives and that we can learn to anticipate and manage major turning points in our careers. In the process we take a fresh look at the whole concept of a career in today's dynamic job market, accepting that things are likely to be a little less predictable than the 'job for life' model of the 1960s and 1970s, with its idea of a career as something that was planned in adolescence and that would unfold in adult life.

The concept of career learning *emphasises the importance of integrating past experience in a coherent and meaningful way so that we can capitalise on future opportunities.*

Throughout this book we have stressed the importance of the workplace as a learning environment, and the opportunities it offers to learn not just about our jobs but also about our role in the team and the wider organisation. This chapter brings together some of these important ideas by putting the spotlight on the concept of *career learning*. This emphasises the importance of integrating past experience in a coherent and meaningful way so that we can capitalise on future opportunities.

The three main topics explored in this chapter are:

- What is a career today? – examines how today's less predictable labour market puts the emphasis on the ability to take advantage of new situations rather than on mapping out a planned route well in advance.

- Key tasks in career learning – looks at how a dynamic approach to learning is vital to successful career management.

- The CV: a passport for learning? – explores the most effective and appropriate ways of presenting learning and experience to potential employers and clients – looking at how you can breathe fresh life into the often rather hackneyed and stilted medium of the *curriculum vitae*.

What is a career today?

Not very long ago a 14- or 15-year-old in secondary school could expect to be approached by their year tutor with the question 'Have you given any thought to a career at all?'. By way of reply, he or she would be expected to volunteer one or more job titles: 'Oh yes sir, I'd like to become a teacher' – or an accountant, a butcher, a banker, a candlestick maker or, just possibly, a sagger-maker's bottom-knocker.[1] As we enter a new century, however, careers lessons are much more likely to stress the statistic that young people leaving full-time education should expect to change their occupation at least twice during their working lives. Given this fundamental shift, does the word 'career' still have any meaning and value? In our view, the answer to this question is intimately connected with a career-long approach to learning and professional development.

---

[1] This was an occupation which apparently flourished in the pottery towns during the Industrial Revolution.

Learning at the crossroads

There have been several points in this book where we have seen that an individual's priorities as a learner are bound up with their position in their lives as a whole. In Chapter 2, for instance, we offered the technique of drawing up a learning lifeline as a method for reflecting on how your own orientation to learning may shift and vary over time.

One graphic illustration of the relationship between learning and other life priorities came in Chapter 1. There we met a group of graduate recruits with a top-flight engineering company who had no interest at all in recording their learning experiences on the job because learning was not a priority for them at that point in their careers. They had finally left full-time study with good degree results and wanted to focus on different aspects of their lives – getting a mortgage on a house, joining a golf club and so on.

In fact, it is by no means unusual for people in their early and mid twenties to see things this way. Adult education courses of every kind and at every academic and vocational level have always found it very difficult if not impossible to attract individuals aged between 20 and 30. While there is no real evidence that this pattern is changing in the context of formal courses, we have encountered some interesting exceptions in the work-based route.

Changing gear in early career – modern apprentices at the Royal United Hospital

As part of a project looking into the implementation of the key skills units in the workplace, we worked with two people in their early twenties who had just started modern apprenticeships as Operating Department Practitioners (ODPs). In itself this is a relatively new occupation. Twenty years ago much of the work of an ODP would have formed part of the responsibility of the theatre nurses. Today, however, ODPs are valued members of the team. They make sure that doctors, anaesthetists and nurses have full access to all the resources and equipment that they need, as and when they need them. ODPs play a key role in ensuring that patients receive a high standard of care throughout their time with the operating department – before the operation, on the operating table and in the recovery room.

This is not an occupation that is likely to be mentioned in a careers lesson, or highlighted as an option by a computer-aided careers guidance package. Nevertheless, there is rarely a shortage of applications when a vacancy is advertised. Typically these applications come from people in their early or mid twenties who have found out about the job through some form of direct contact with the health service. This was true of both of the apprentices we worked with. David[2] had left school with A levels in Ancient History and Art and Design and originally joined the hospital as a porter. Jane, who also left school with arts A levels, was making a bigger career change. At first she had taken a job at a cement works, becoming production manager responsible – amongst other things – for the firm's ISO 9000 quality control system. Her mother had been a nurse, however, and Jane had always been keen to work in the health sector: originally she planned to join the Ambulance Service.

Both of these young people had entered a two-year training programme at comparatively unusual points in their lives. David was married and keen to start a family. Jane was also in a long-term relationship and shared a mortgage with her partner. Despite this, she had been prepared to take a noticeable cut in her income so that she could learn a completely new set of skills and values.

David and Jane are examples of people making their way in life who have been prepared to change their occupation after only three or four years out of school or college. At one time this would have been a highly unusual pattern for anyone leaving full-time education with recognised qualifications. But perhaps it no longer makes sense to think in terms of typical 'career patterns'.

Conventional views about career development

Throughout the immediate post-war era, in fact up to the 'energy crisis' of the mid 1970s, western economies enjoyed an unusually long period of sustained growth and stability. Many of our conventional ideas of how an individual's career might unfold date back to this period. There was a

---

[2] The names 'David' and 'Jane' are pseudonyms used in the published write-up of the project at the request of the hospital.

comfortable assumption that people's working lives would progress steadily and undramatically through a series of easy-to-predict stages. It can be quite salutary to look back to that period through the eyes of those who were involved in careers education and guidance at the time.

Unquestionably the most influential writer on the theory of careers guidance during this period was the American, Donald Super. Over a number of years he gradually refined and extended a model of the career development process which argued that our working lives go through a series of five age-related stages (see Figure 11.1, p. 216).

The level of predictability implied by Super's model depends on an almost totally static view of the world of work. From our present perspective, only too aware of the power of demographic, technological and cultural change, Super's cosy stages may seem almost incredibly banal. But 30 years ago there was a real vogue for popular books on this theme. Titles like Sheehy's *Passages: Predictable Crises of Adult Life* and Levinson's *The Seasons of a Man's Life* sold by the bucketful.

Apart from the failure to realise that the safe and settled labour market of the sixties and early seventies was actually something of an aberration, there are two characteristics of these life-stage models which mark them out as very much a product of their time:

- Firstly, they assume that the basic shape of most people's lives will follow pretty much the same 'normal' pattern. At the time there was definitely a prescriptive flavour to this assumption. It was felt that this was how careers *should* progress. Major deviations from the norm – such as people who changed their jobs frequently throughout their working lives – were seen as a problem. Government agencies felt that they should do something to help these poor unfortunates.

- Secondly, there was an assumption that a lot of the hard work in career development terms was done quite early on in life. The view was that careers were planned well in advance – preferably in secondary school. In fact Super produced a psychometric inventory of 'career maturity in adolescence' which assumed that 'planfulness' was the most important factor in settling in early to a successful and satisfactory career.

Figure 11.1 Super's life-career stages

Growth
(Birth to 14)

As Super saw it, during childhood we gradually build up a picture of the jobs that we might do – in the first instance by identifying with our parents and teachers.

↓

Exploration
(15 to 24)

Super thought that the key career tasks during adolescence and early adulthood were those of building up a clear picture of our interests, capabilities and values and trying out a number of possible job roles – at first through fantasy and later in reality.

↓

Establishment
(25 to 44)

Now the emphasis was on securing a permanent place in the individual's chosen occupation. Super suggested that unskilled workers might occasionally change their jobs early on during this stage but that professionals would generally stay put.

↓

Maintenance
(45 to 64)

For Super middle age was basically a holding operation. As he put it: 'Little new ground is broken, but there is continuation along established lines.'

↓

Decline
(65 and on)

Super's view was that during retirement men and women become observers rather than participants in the world of work.

Adapted from: Super, 1957 and Super and Bohn, 1971

This focus on adolescence may seem rather paradoxical today but it reflects the fact that, then as now, most 'careers specialists' worked in schools, and research psychologists have always found it easier to study children and teenagers. As Barrie Hopson and Mike Scally once put it:

To look at a typical textbook in psychology you could think that human development stopped at age 21.

The Adult as a Developing Person (Hopson and Scally, 1979)

Challenging convention – career success in adulthood

All three of the authors of this book joined the labour market during the late seventies, just as conventional assumptions over what constituted a career were being challenged by rapidly rising unemployment. In fact on leaving university Eddy got a job working for Donald Super at the National Institute for Careers Education and Counselling (NICEC) in Cambridge. My first publication – with Don – was concerned with the factors involved in successful career management in adulthood (Super and Knasel, 1981).

This arose out of a small research project funded by Canada Employment and Immigration. This government agency was concerned at the number of unskilled and semi-skilled workers who, rather than settling down into a steady job, seemed to make a career out of changing their employer on a more or less regular basis. In fact 'persistent job changers' were receiving quite a lot of attention at that point. In England, Nicola Cherry had just published a paper suggesting that this strategy might not be a problem at all. She had found that people who did 'play the field' in this way often actually benefited, both financially and in terms of a number of psychological measures. The task for Don and myself was to investigate whether there were any characteristics which seemed to lead to career success amongst people aged 18–30.

I carried out a series of in-depth interviews with 48 blue-collar workers. Analysing the transcripts, I found that many of the statements made by these experienced workers fitted into a category which had not emerged from Don's previous work with American high school students. Here are some of the things they said:

I think that you can look back over a job that you've held for four or five years and see a progression in how you react to certain circumstances. When I look back at this job I think I've lost some of my patience and some of my niceness – I'm not totally naïve anymore. I'm more adamant about things.

I think every job to me was an experience. You have your ups and downs but I'm glad I've had the chance to do all these jobs.

She talked me into getting a job at the University and that was a turning point for me. I started to realise that a job could be interesting as well as bring home money. Before that I'd just seen a job as something to keep the money rolling in.

I learned a great deal in those two years. I think I grew a lot. I mean I'm glad to have this political knowledge. I learned a great deal about life's hypocrisy.

In our paper Don and I referred to this category as 'reflection on experience'. The important point was that the people who made these statements had been in the labour market for some time. They had a career history that they could look back on and, as the quotations show, they had learned valuable lessons from it. Indeed, listening to these people it became clear that this process of looking back at past experience was at least as important as the process of looking forwards and planning ahead which was the only option open to the high school students of previous studies. Through reflection, the adults could focus on significant learning episodes; they could find meaning and coherence in a succession of jobs which to an outsider might seem quite incoherent and illogical.

This perspective exposed another assumption in the conventional view of a career as a succession of events planned in advance. A planned career is one where it makes sense to talk of the individual making *progress* towards certain goals. It may be possible to gauge how far one has moved from A to B, rather like judging the distance travelled from one town to another on a map. The adults I interviewed, on the other hand, seemed to have experienced careers which had *evolved* rather than progressed. Few of them had any very clear idea of where they expected to be in five years time. They did, however, know where they had been. The lessons they had learned along the way seemed to have given them a clearer idea of how they would weigh up any new opportunities that the future might have to offer.

Interesting times

Back in 1979, when most of my interviews were carried out, it may have made sense to draw a distinction between blue-collar workers – who might be expected to experience the kind of 'retrospective career' where reflection is more important than planning – and executives and professionals who might still imagine that they could chart out their future path decades in advance. In practice, however, reflection on experience is bound to have helped them to make adjustments as they went along and the move to flatter organisational structures, as companies stripped out the 'dead wood' of middle and senior management during the 1980s, meant that many senior staff who might have expected to enjoy the 'maintenance' stage found themselves experiencing what we might now call 'interesting times'!

Balancing life roles – towards a portfolio career?

There is another sense in which white-collar careers have come closer to blue-collar patterns over the nineties. In the past, as well as changing jobs more frequently, unskilled and semi-skilled workers were more likely to hold more than one job at a time – say painting and decorating during the day, but not necessarily every day, and working at a petrol station a few evenings a week. In contrast, the stereotypical middle class manager held down one nine-to-five, five-days-a-week position.

Now, with the increasing emergence of what are often called 'portfolio careers', the position for managers and executives shows signs of becoming more flexible. *Job-sharing* has meant that part-time employment is no longer necessarily seen as an oddity and an increasing number of well qualified people are learning to balance work with other life roles – parenting, voluntary work, part-time study and so on.

Job-sharing

As part of our work in the health service we recently came across a GP practice in the South West of England where the staff had gone a long way towards putting the idea of 'portfolio careers' into action. The practice involves seven experienced doctors, both male and female, who between them share the equivalent of four full-time posts. Not one of the doctors works in medicine full time but five of them have additional sources of income – two run arts and crafts businesses, one has a smallholding, another has interests in leisure and tourism and so on.

Alternatively, some professionals are coming to mix more than one way of earning a living. So the idea of the 'gentleman farmer' is beginning to resurface in agriculture, with professionals earning some income from a smallholding but also continuing to keep their hands in as architects, accountants, journalists and so on – maybe three days a week. There is also a growing trend towards interim management.

Interim management

The nineties have seen a rise in the number of executives moving into self-employment. An interesting phenomenon is that of 'interim management'. This is a practice, which seems to have originated in manufacturing, whereby senior managers take short-term contracts to carry out a specific job in a company. This might mean taking over a management function for a defined period of time or leading a specific project. Interim managers are self-employed and a number of agencies have sprung up which bring together client organisations and independent executives. The majority of interim managers are aged over 45. By no means all of them work all round the year: for many interim management offers an attractive form of what might once have been called 'semi-retirement' where they enjoy a reasonable income but also give attention to other activities – travel, leisure interests, community work and so on.

Source: www.workingfutures.com

Key tasks in career learning

Notions of career planning based on a once-and-for-all (or even once-in-a-while) review of the options and priorities are weak because both the options and the priorities will change. The requirement is that people need repeatedly to review career choices and transitions, with thought and care. All this argues for supporting people through a lifelong process of career-related thinking and rethinking, action and new action.

A Career-Learning Theory (Law, 1996)

So if traditional ideas of career development are no longer an appropriate way of describing how a person's experience of work evolves and unfolds, how should we view our careers? Our own views about this are best summed up by the phrase 'career learning'. This is a term which has recently been introduced by Bill Law, a former colleague at NICEC. He used it to refer to the way in which 'people learn to manage their careers'.

For us, the appeal of this perspective is that it casts career management as essentially a learning process. It implies that the people with an active and dynamic approach to learning will be best able to make sense of their career experiences. They will be able to use the understanding of themselves and of the nature of work that they gain from these learning episodes to make soundly based decisions as they are faced with new opportunities. They will be able to draw meaning from their reflections and pose critical questions about their own capabilities and achievements, and about any opportunities that they create or which happen to come their way.

Career learning vs lifelong and lifetime learning

It may be helpful to make a distinction between career learning and the perhaps rather more familiar phrase 'lifelong learning'. Certainly there is some potential for confusion between the two as both stress that learning happens at every age, and at every decision and transition point. Semantically, however, 'career learning' puts a greater emphasis on the work role and on the active process of finding a pattern within an individual's experiences and opportunities and suggests a clearer focus on the management of decision and transition points.

Both career learning and lifelong learning can be readily distinguished from 'lifetime learning', a phrase which in practice is most frequently used by educational policy makers. In the UK, government agencies see the aims of lifetime learning in terms of making formal education and training provision available to men and women throughout their working lives. This emphasis is illustrated in a fairly recent official publication which defines the aims of lifetime learning as being to:

. . . provide a coherent package of policies and activities which encourage individuals to invest in skills.

Individual Commitment to Learning – Making it Happen (Wilson, 1995)

Wilson goes on to state that these policies and activities should address:

- motivation and awareness of the benefits of learning
- information, advice and guidance on learning opportunities and support structures
- paying for learning, putting the individual in control and access
- assessment (including accreditation of prior learning) and learning opportunities
- recognition of achievement (e.g. qualifications and reward).

In terms of the three Es the stress here is clearly on the economic justification for learning. In contrast, 'career learning' has a much more individual focus: it is relevant to discussions of human powers rather than government strategy

Two key tasks

At heart there are two key tasks which must be addressed in career learning: reflection on experience and managing dynamic situations.

Reflection on experience

Looking back, it is clear that the workers Eddy interviewed back in 1979 were often able to talk about their career histories as a series of learning episodes. They highlighted certain decisions and transition points as having particular importance to them and were able to say what they had gained from them, using the skills of reflection described in Chapter 6. Subconsciously they had sifted through their experiences – Bill Law puts the spotlight on 'sifting' as a key career learning skill – and had left many of their most routine experiences out of their commentaries. This is how they were able to construct a 'retrospective career'.

Interestingly, these interviewees tended to concentrate primarily on what they had learned about the world of work rather than what they had learned about their own abilities and capabilities. It is clear, however, that this kind of personal audit is an important part of the career learning process. It is how we can be confident about what we have to offer to the job market.

Priorities in a personal career audit

Recently we have been involved in the development of a series of open learning modules for a company called Working Futures which offers a range of careers services marketed over the Internet. The module titled *Maximising Your Potential* includes a career audit designed to help clients to reflect on the experiences, skills and abilities they bring to the job market. The main topics covered are:

- work experience
- achievements
- transferable skills
- work values
- work satisfaction
- work style.

Managing dynamic situations

Bill Law and Tony Watts argued that one of the most important aims of careers education and guidance programmes should be to help school leavers to 'make career decisions wisely'. Today, this is precisely what is required of us throughout our adult lives. Whenever we are faced with an unexpected job offer – or an unexpected redundancy offer! – it is vital to look at the situation critically on the basis of well-grounded information. Much of this information will, in fact, come from our reflection on our experiences.

Recognising the importance of these two key tasks adds an additional facet to our picture of the learning process. Both of them draw extensively on the skills and attitudes that have been reviewed throughout this book. The relevance of a dynamic approach to learning to the area of careers shows that learning is not only a process which goes on throughout our lives: it also offers the key to bringing structure and coherence to our lives as a whole.

The CV: a passport for learning?

Finally in this chapter we look at what could be regarded as a third career learning task which has a part to play in gaining success in the job market – presenting what you have learned and achieved to potential employers or, if you are running your own business, potential clients.

There are a number of different ways in which you may be able to demonstrate the relevance of your skills and abilities – for instance through letters, interviews, assessment centres, presentations and so on – but one of the main vehicles remains the *curriculum vitae* or CV. We have already looked in detail at devices for recording and analysing your experiences, including reflective diaries and critical incidents techniques. These are, however, devices which the learner compiles for his or her own use; they themselves are the audience. In compiling a CV, however, the audience is a third party who remains to be convinced that the person whose skills and abilities are showcased genuinely does have something to offer. In many ways you can think of a CV as a piece of personal marketing literature.

Too often CVs are intensely boring documents – boring to produce and boring to read.

Too often CVs are intensely boring documents – boring to produce and boring to read. And yet convention, in the form of time honoured selection and recruitment practices, means that the CV remains the format which most closely resembles a recognised learning passport.

The CV industry

One of the main reasons why CVs have become such predictable and, paradoxically, impersonal documents is that a whole industry has grown up around providing tips and guidelines on the best ways of writing and presenting them.

For years courses and booklets have been available which promise to reveal the secrets of how to produce two or three sparkling pages that will unlock the door to a new career. In some ways the situation resembles an arms race. People go on these courses and buy these books because they believe that the techniques they learn will give them a competitive edge. The more successful the industry becomes, the harder the people who earn a living from it will hunt for new presentational tricks and gimmicks. The result is that there are quite noticeable 'fashions' in the way that CVs are put together. These trends have very little to do with the achievements of the people sending in the CVs, or even the requirements of the HR managers who have to read them, but rather a lot to do with the cunning and ingenuity of the trainers and authors working in the field.

At the moment there are two main styles of CV in circulation:

- **The 'historical' CV.** This is still probably the most common format. It involves laying out your career history as a continuous sequence of jobs, backed up with notes about the expertise and experience gained in each one. Clearly it is most appropriate to people whose sequence of jobs appears immediately logical and appropriate to a third party. The fact that it is assumed that this is what recruitment specialists will be looking for perhaps illustrates the extent to which we are still locked into the notion of a 'planned' career.

- **The 'skills' CV.** Here the individual's experiences are grouped together as a series of skills and competencies which are on offer at the moment, with the positions in which they were learned given second priority. This style is often recommended to those who are changing direction or moving into consultancy.

There is nothing intrinsically wrong with either of these approaches. Skilfully applied to the right situations either could be an effective way for an individual to market their talents. The rot sets in, however, when you put the language used in specimen CVs under the microscope. Here are three examples of profile statements taken from genuine recent materials:

Phillip Salthrop: Customer-sensitive, profit-driven and focused team leader and player. Achieves results in large-scale organisations, internationally and in the UK.

Shirley Holmes: HR professional with wide ranging experience of business in a European manufacturing environment – operating at the forefront of change in customer-oriented business culture.

Roger David: Board Director who develops and turns round businesses. Team builder and team member who enjoys challenging the status quo. Makes a 'constructive difference' by initiating and delivering strategic solutions to business problems.

Apart from gaining the impression that these individuals have physically swallowed a dictionary of 'management speak', what could you possibly learn about these people from these statements? Could you imagine actually meeting any of them? Our view is that this stilted and mannered language would seriously undermine the value of the CV as a communication device: it acts as a buffer between the writer – who is trying to present what he or she has to offer in a favourable light – and the reader who wants to get a genuine and authentic feel for the person who is making the application. This is why CVs are often such a chore. The irony is that capturing the positive highlights of what you have learned to date should be a really enjoyable experience!

Your personal brand – beyond the CV?

In Chapter 1 we introduced the idea of your 'personal brand'. This idea owes much to Tom Peters, who argues that 'to be in business today, our most important job is to be head marketer for the brand called You'. For Peters the starting point is to identify the qualities and characteristics that are distinctive about you – things like always delivering work on time, completing projects within budgets or providing a reliable service.

Our own CV guidelines

Having criticised the CV industry, it is only fair that we should close this chapter by offering our own five key steps to producing a CV which genuinely does communicate what you have to offer:

- **Give an accurate picture of yourself**. Choose the format and language which best suits your own personal style. Try to give a real flavour of the person the readers would meet if they were to ask to see you face-to-face. Think critically whenever you are tempted to use a buzzword or convenient sound bite. Would you be impressed if you were the reader?

- **Know your audience**. There is nothing wrong with producing a new CV tailored to the specific vacancy or tender. In fact, doing this is a good way of keeping your CV up-to-date; an accurate reflection of the person you are now rather than the person you were three or four years ago.

- **Think of how your strengths may transfer to other contexts**. Take care not to use language that is specific to particular situations and organisations. Instead, concentrate on showing how you can transfer what you have learned from one situation to another.

- **Be genuine**. People can almost certainly tell if you dress up your experience in an exaggerated way. Be honest about your achievements – but do make sure that you stress your strengths.

- **Write clearly**. People are not impressed by over-elaborate language. Use a clear, direct and straightforward writing style.

Overall, it may be helpful to think seriously about your CV as marketing material. How do the professionals do it? Look through some newspapers and magazines to find the advertisements that capture – and then hold – your interest. Our guess would be that they will be the ones which are written in adult-to-adult language, which keep the level of hype and hard sell well under control and which make a genuine attempt to show why their product or service stands out from the crowd.

In the new world of work and portfolio careers such thinking may offer other ways of presenting yourself that go beyond the traditional CV. It suggests that everything you do should reflect your basic values and beliefs – that you will market yourself best by being yourself.

The last chapter takes our views of learning a step further and asks how learning can help us prepare for the future.

12 Learning for democracy?

> The model of transmission of information from teacher to student . . . is no longer sufficient in a society where knowledge is changing rapidly, and the skills needed both at work and in our social lives are becoming increasingly complex.
>
> *Technology, Open Learning and Distance Education* (Bates, 1995)

In the opening chapter of this book we argued that the unprecedented amount of knowledge and information available today places ever increasing demands on our powers of learning. Now, in this closing chapter, we return to this theme, looking in particular at the challenge posed to our ability to learn collectively.

The organisational and social structures in which we live and work today are 'information rich' – a vast store of knowledge is potentially available to every one of us, and we need to be confident in our ability to act on this information in making collective decisions. This chapter argues that, in consequence, we need both to develop our personal capabilities as learners and to develop our collective power of learning – so that together we can learn from the collective mistakes of the past.

The chapter explores:

- Can we learn collectively? – how our collective knowledge has outstripped our collective wisdom and understanding, raising questions about our ability to cope with the explosion of information.

- Improving learning at work – the key tasks in 'learning design' and the need to raise the professionalism of trainers and coaches.

- A career in learning? – finally, we sign off with a glance at how a dynamic approach to learning can enrich not just our working lives but every aspect of our adult experience.

Can we learn collectively?

Throughout this book we have been very positive about the power and potential of human learning. In this final chapter, however, we are going to strike an important note of caution. We have absolute confidence in the potential of each and every one of us as individual learners. We are much less confident, however, in our ability to learn collectively. And yet developing our ability to make collective decisions and to make intelligent use of our huge accumulation of collective knowledge poses one of the most significant challenges that we shall face through the new century. Over the next few pages we shall examine how the structure of our organisations and our society places great demands on our capacity as questioning learners. Can we bring the same critical faculties that we can develop as individuals to the collective task of shared decision making? There is a great deal riding on the answer to this question.

Learning and the democratic process

Individual and collective learning reinforces the informed, conscious and discriminating choices that underpin democracy

A Declaration on Learning (Learning Declaration Group, 1998)

In Chapters 1 and 4 we saw the very real sense in which Paulo Freire's work in adult literacy was concerned with learning for empowerment. Unless the people he was working with could show that they had learned to read they would not be able to vote in national elections.

In itself this illustrates the close relationship that has always existed between learning and the democratic process. In Victorian England one of the main arguments advanced against the extension of the right to vote to the whole adult population was the conviction that the 'uneducated masses' would be too ignorant to use their vote intelligently. The development of state education was largely a response to this concern – and also to the awareness that developing industries required more informed and aware workers. It has always been accepted that democracy depends on voters who have at least a basic understanding of the issues that divide the parties, and the ability to ask relevant questions about the politicians who are up for election.

This is as true today as it has ever been. For our society to function we are expected to hold informed opinions on a wide variety of subjects. Topics like the introduction of a common European currency, the arguments for and against genetic engineering and the relationship between crime and punishment involve a wealth of information and a range of conflicting theoretical arguments. And yet how many members of the public who respond to radio phone-ins have a genuine critical understanding of topics like these? And how many of us have the time and inclination to find out more?

The need for informed consumers

It is not just the formal electoral process that relies on our knowledge and understanding. The decisions that we make as purchasers and consumers can also have major implications for the economy and the environment. Frequently, however, the choices that we make are based on quite minimal amounts of information.

The food industry provides a good example of this. In their lively and thought-provoking book, *The Food System*, Geoff Tansey and Peter Worsley distinguished between a number of 'key actors' who have a part to play in a chain of events leading up to the presence of a meal on our dinner table – farmers, processors, retailers and consumers (Figure 12.1).

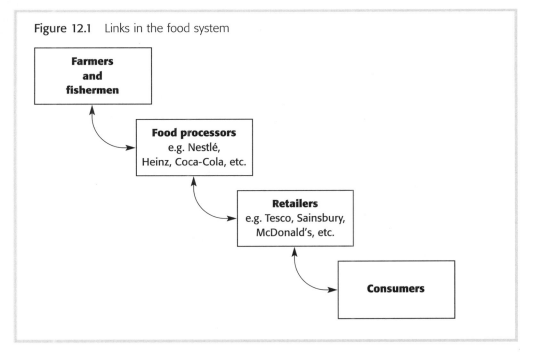

Figure 12.1   Links in the food system

The purchasing decisions made at the corner shop or in the burger bar make a big, but indirect, difference to the actions of the first actors in the chain – the farmers. In turn, the business decisions made by farmers affect how they use their land, impacting on the habitats available to wildlife. This means that the choices that we make on our weekly trips to the supermarket can and do have long-term implications for bio-diversity and for the 'balance of nature' across our planet as a whole. And yet market research shows that relatively few of us have any detailed knowledge of what we are buying. For most of us an orange is an orange irrespective of where, when and how it was grown.

Oranges are not the only citrus fruit

Market research surveys have consistently shown that UK consumers, of all ages and social classes, have very little knowledge of even some of the most commonplace items on their shopping lists. When asked to name three different types of orange we are likely to focus on the country of origin. The assumption is that one Spanish orange is pretty much the same as another – British consumers simply do not realise that different varieties of orange vary considerably in terms of factors such as juiciness, sweetness and acidity. Supermarkets have also found that most of us have only the haziest knowledge of when oranges grown in Israel or South Africa are likely to be in season. Instead, it seems that we are much more influenced by an unblemished appearance than any real knowledge of the fruit we are buying. As one baffled Spanish grower apparently put it:

The English must eat their oranges with their eyes.

In our view the problem is not so much an unwillingness to understand the issues involved, more a consequence of the fact that today there is just too much information available for any one person to make sense of it all.

The information explosion

We introduced *The World Turned Upside Down*, Christopher Hill's classic study of political radicalism following the English Civil War, in Chapter 4. In many ways Hill's 'hero' is the 'digger' and 'true leveller', Gerard Winstanley. Winstanley had a vision of an ideal society based on communal ownership. In 1649 he founded a community at St George's Hill, just outside London, to demonstrate what this could mean in practice. He also distributed a tract, *The Law of Freedom* (1652), which amounted to a manifesto for a reformed society in which private property had been abolished.

Winstanley worked through his ideas in remarkable detail. One of his most original suggestions was concerned with how information could be put at everybody's fingertips. In a proposal which in some ways anticipates the access to research made possible by the Internet, Winstanley recommended that each parish should elect two 'Postmasters'. Their role would be to collect and report statistical information about the health and welfare of the community and also to publicise information and inventions from other parts of the country supplied to them through a network of regional centres.

Winstanley's aim was that this system would give everyone immediate access to any new breakthrough or discovery as soon as it happened. It would also mean the abolition of trade secrets; there would be a 'commonwealth' of knowledge that could be acted on by any citizen.

Christopher Hill argues that Winstanley's ideas were practical and realistic at the time that they were written. His postmaster system, however, does not seem workable today, given the sheer volume of data and information that is now in circulation. In medicine alone the weight of research published is such that governments are obliged to spend considerable sums of money on systems which make the most significant findings available in a distilled and digestible form. Winstanley looked forward to a time when we could all carry the latest information on any subject in our heads. Today there is no possibility that an individual doctor could keep pace with every development even in their own professional specialty.

The NHS R&D Strategy

During the early nineties the UK government established what it claimed was the most ambitious attempt anywhere in the world to provide a coherent national infrastructure for coordinating and communicating health research and development. At the heart of this R&D strategy was a perception that:

Strongly held views based on belief rather than sound information still exert too much influence in healthcare.

Research for Health (Department of Health, 1991)

As part of this strategy the Department of Health funded two national centres whose function was to provide reliable overviews of research findings in key areas, so that doctors could have access to them in a format compatible with the limited time they have available for reading and reflection.

The need for collective learning

Since Winstanley's time there has been an explosion in the amount of knowledge and information available to us collectively as a society. It is no longer possible to think in terms of the 'renaissance man', adept in every area of the arts and sciences. The result is that knowledge has become fragmented; individuals specialise in ever more closely defined areas. The full range of knowledge can only be held collectively.

Collective knowledge gives us great benefits and advantages. Without it we would not have the great technical and scientific developments that have flowed in a constant stream since the Industrial Revolution. But it is questionable whether we have yet developed the collective wisdom and understanding necessary to cope with this knowledge.

> *The full range of knowledge can only be held collectively.*

This point is raised in Cecil Lewis' book *Sagittarius Rising*, an account of his experiences in the First World War. Lewis lied about his age and joined the Royal Flying Corps when he was just 17. By the summer of 1916, still aged only 18, he found himself flying solo reconnaissance missions over enemy lines during the infamous battle of the Somme. Here he reflects on what happened one evening as he headed back from the trenches. It was an episode that was to stay with him for the rest of his life:

As I came back from the lines one evening, I saw to the north of Thiepval a long creeping wraith of yellow mist. I stared for a moment before I realised: Gas! Then, instinctively, although I was a mile above the earth, I pulled back the stick to climb higher, away from the horror.

In the light westerly wind it slid slowly down the German trenches, creeping panther-like over the scarred earth, curling down into dugouts, coiling and uncoiling in the wind's whim. Men were dying there, under me, from a whiff of it: not dying quickly, not even maimed or shattered, but dying whole, retching and vomiting blood and guts; and those who lived would be wrecks with seared, poisoned lungs, rotten for life.

I stared at the yellow drift, hypnotized. I can see it at this moment as clearly as I could that day, for it remains with me as the most pregnant memory of the war. It was, in fact, the symbol of our enlightened twentieth century; science, in the pursuit of knowledge, being exploited by a world without standards or scruples, spiritually bankrupt.

This image of the Somme, and of the 'industrialisation' of warfare, is a reminder that many of the catastrophes of the twentieth century were due to deliberate misuse of knowledge. It highlights the point that there is a moral dimension to the application of learning. But it would be a mistake to put all of the blame on the likes of Adolph Hitler, Josef Stalin and Pol Pot, or their misguided henchmen. Comparable damage has been caused by mistakes that have been made simply because we have lacked the collective understanding to question the use made of our technology.

A good example here is the development of intensive agriculture. Farming methods – particularly in crop production – were transformed during the second half of the twentieth century, resulting in yields that were hitherto unimaginable. A big factor was the use of fertilisers and pesticides to promote the growth of crops but it is important not to underestimate the impact of mechanisation. The introduction of tractors changed the way that farmers could work the land. In turn, economies of scale encouraged the use of larger and more efficient machines – which allowed farmers to work much bigger fields. Hedgerows and other field boundaries, which supported a rich variety of wildlife including birds and mammals, were stripped out: the impact on biodiversity has been little short of disastrous. Since 1945 the UK has lost:

- over 250 000 miles of hedgerow
- 95% of herb-rich meadows
- 80% of downland grassland
- 50% of ancient woodland.

As a result there have been major declines in the numbers of many species of mammals, birds, insects and flowering plants. To give just a few examples, the numbers of grey partridges are down by 82 per cent, bullfinches by 75 per cent and skylarks by 58 per cent.

The irony is that farmers themselves have not really had any long-term benefits from all of this. Increased efficiency has not necessarily led to increased profits – in fact profit margins have been squeezed throughout the last 20 years.

Is there something we can learn?

Analysing collective situations like this is not a matter of apportioning blame. We would not expect any of the key actors in the food industry chain to carry the can for results which have been as unintentional as they have been unanticipated. But there are lessons that can be gained when such issues are put in the spotlight; particularly in terms of the challenges which confront our readiness and ability to learn collectively.

Of course the example of intensive agriculture does highlight some of the pressures that are put on us as individual learners in our present society. As individuals, farmers have been required to learn a huge range of techniques and a wide variety of new knowledge just to keep in step with developments. Relatively few of them have been in a position to take in the whole picture or to ask critical questions about the wider impact of these developments. And, although many consumers are now actively trying to find out more about the food on supermarket shelves, until recently very few of us made it a priority to reflect on the full price that we might be paying for choice and convenience. Most of us are only consumers for a fraction of our waking lives – and there are so many other things for us to learn about in our other roles.

Nevertheless, it is impossible to escape the conclusion that at the individual level we have not always asked the right questions about the food that we eat – and about many of the other issues that we face as a society. Democracy depends on empowered, active learners and more can be done to encourage us all to improve our performance at this level. In a moment we shall move on to look at some of the priorities in ensuring that the workplace can play a part in this.

But collective situations also demand collective learning. In one sense we have been very successful as collective learners. In terms of volume we have gathered an overwhelming store of data and information. At the individual level, however, Chapter 8 emphasised the importance of critical questioning in moving from the accumulation of knowledge to real understanding and wisdom. The collective equivalent of this phase of the learning curve, where together we can learn from our shared experiences, seems relatively undeveloped. Too often the mechanisms for shared critical reflection on issues which are bound up in collective knowledge have proved weak and ineffective.

Stated in this way the problem of collective learning may seem very abstract. But it is highly relevant to many of the practical social and political issues that we face today. We will only learn from the mistakes of the past – particularly the mistakes of the twentieth century – if we can apply what we know about the power of human learning to the way that we structure our society.

Progress is possible

Collective learning at the social and political level may seem a tall order but we may be able to find grounds for optimism in the progress that has been made in addressing similar issues in organisations.

In Chapter 8 we looked at the impetus given to learning in the workplace by the advent of the total quality movement. W. Edwards Deming was one of the key figures in establishing the concern with quality. Initially his message fell on stony ground in the United States but it was eagerly accommodated in post-war Japan. Late on in his career Deming published his book *Out of the Crisis* in which he voiced his frustration with the failure of American industry to learn the same lessons as its competitors. He was particularly irritated by the prevalent focus on short-term profits which he thought ran counter to the development of a truly successful organisation:

Performance of management should be measured by potential to stay in business, to protect investment, to ensure future dividends and jobs through improvement of product and service for the future, not by the quarterly dividend.

Out of the Crisis (Deming, 1986)

He added that an open and active approach to learning would be required if things were to move forward:

Long-term commitment to new learning and new philosophy is required of any management that seeks transformation.

He recognised that this represented a significant challenge to entrenched attitudes and established systems:

Only transformation of the American style of management, and of government relations with industry can halt the decline and give American industry a chance to lead the world again.

At the time of writing – early 2000 – the American economy does seem to have achieved a measure of the stability and growth that Deming aspired to. Many factors have been at play here, but some of the credit must go to those managers and professionals who have accepted the agenda proposed by figures like Deming, Moss Kanter and Schonberger. There are several organisations where 'defensive management' is now less prevalent and where a climate has been created which encourages a measure of shared critical questioning at the team level.

Can similar progress be achieved at the broader social and political level?

In 1944 Max Horkheimer and Theodor Adorno reflected on the rise and fall of fascism in their native Germany while in exile in the United States. In *The Dialectic of Enlightenment* – a seminal book which has profoundly influenced writers such as Freire and Habermas – they highlighted the crucial contradiction in the knowledge explosion. This contradiction is that knowledge can be put just as readily to the service of mass deception and 'blind domination' as to the service of positive, shared enlightenment.

This book has set out our firm belief – introduced in Chapter 1, explored in Chapters 4 and 6 and fully developed in Chapter 8 – that the ability to question critically the multiplicity of available knowledge is crucial to challenging mass deception. Our hope is that if enough people become powerful, questioning learners, then the chances of shared understanding and wisdom increase. Ultimately this will depend on whether, as adults, we each have the chance to live and work in an environment which encourages learning through responsible freedom.

To make progress towards collective learning we need a learning environment, not just in schools and colleges but also in the workplace.

Many factors will influence this environment, several beyond the scope of this book. But our primary focus has been on learning in the workplace, and we believe that to make progress towards collective learning we need a learning environment, not just in schools and colleges but also in the workplace. So, as we come towards the end of this final chapter, we will look more closely at the role you can play in creating and sustaining this environment.

Improving learning at work

This has been a book about learning rather than teaching or training. Quite deliberately, we have kept the focus on the active role of the individual in exploiting his or her power as a learner. It is crucial now, though, to go one step further and discuss the role that individuals play within the organisation in establishing an environment in which learning can flourish. As a manager you will have a strategic part to play in creating and sustaining this environment.

Priorities in learning design

A few years ago the Department for Education and Employment asked us to review a series of seven projects they had commissioned from Industry Training Organisations (ITOs) on planning and implementing workplace learning. The resulting publication (Rossetti, Meed and Knasel, 1996) highlighted a number of core tasks in 'learning design' that were shared across this wide range of industries – from estate agency to steel making. Our experience suggests that the state of the art has only moved on quite gradually and that the four priorities we raised in *Learning by Design* remain valid for the majority of managers interested in enhancing the quality of learning opportunities available to the people who work in their organisations.

The four priorities were:

- Promoting workplace learning.
- Presenting learners with meaningful tasks.
- Encouraging the transfer of learning.
- Integrating different learning opportunities.

Promoting workplace learning

Sadly, our review showed that in too many companies and too many industries there is still a need to promote the value of the workplace as a learning environment. Managers have an important responsibility in setting the tone: encouraging learning and demonstrating that they are learning themselves. There is still some way to go in establishing the unique value of the workplace – managers need to recognise the distinction between planned and incidental learning and to encourage their staff both to plan formal opportunities and to help their colleagues to reflect on – and learn from – incidental opportunities as and when they crop up. But there are some encouraging signs. As we went to press the Campaign for Learning ran a national 'learning at work day'. This was covered by virtually every national newspaper including the *Financial Times* and the *Daily Mirror* which ran a special learning supplement. Thousands of organisations undertook to create new learning opportunities for their staff.

Presenting learners with meaningful tasks

The projects that we reviewed showed that it is important for people near the beginning of a learning curve to have the experience of carrying out complete tasks in the workplace. Too often trainees are only allowed part of the picture: they do not have the chance to see through an activity that would be recognised as meaningful by experienced workers in the field – tasks they would see as the major building blocks of the job. As another report put it:

Learners constantly fed on a diet of easily digestible 'chopped up tasks' may sometimes never learn to chew or integrate all of the sub-skills into one complex whole.

Thinking and Learning at Work (Blagg and Lewis, 1993)

There is a clear connection between this priority and the notion of learning episodes. An exclusively atomistic approach to training where, as Blagg and Lewis put it, tasks are 'chopped up' in an artificial way limits the value of the experience as an opportunity for critical reflection.

Encouraging the transfer of learning

The ITOs reported a widespread concern that individuals are often slow to transfer what they have learned to new situations. In the security industry it was found that learners could apply their knowledge and skills more appropriately if their colleagues took the trouble to explain the concepts that underpin an activity rather than just the process needed to complete it. In other words, 'deep' approaches may be more successful in this context than a focus on 'surface' learning.

Integrating different learning opportunities

A related priority. This seems to be one of the weakest areas of provision at the moment. Many training programmes include both an 'on-the-job' and an 'off-the-job' element. Frequently there is a lack of communication between the trainers and lecturers working off-the-job and the coaches working on-the-job. Individual learners are then faced with the task of making the connections between the two types of experience for themselves, with relatively little support and guidance.

Improving the quality of learning support

At one time the learning support available in the workplace was characterised as 'sitting by Nellie'. New recruits would be sat down next to an experienced hand, who would be expected to show them the ropes. Typically the situation would be highly informal and ad hoc. 'Nellies' were rarely given any support or training in the role. Often they were not even asked if they minded doing it. As one trade union representative at a manufacturing plant once said to us:

New people used to be told to go and sit by so-and-so. No one ever told so-and-so that they were expected to help the new trainee – let alone how they could best go about it.

This traditional situation was often highly unsatisfactory. In many instances the 'old hands' simply passed on bad working practices. In extreme cases, perhaps in an attempt to 'get back' at management, they would even deliberately give the newcomer false or misleading advice.

Enter the workplace coach

As we saw in Chapter 9, in an increasing number of organisations 'Nellie' is now regarded as a 'coach' or 'mentor'. And the system works in management as well as on the shop-floor. The aim is to cash in on his or her natural skills in supporting another person whilst acknowledging how this makes a valid and valuable contribution to the organisation. Today's coach or mentor will probably have the chance to attend the occasional workshop designed to help them think through their approach to the role.

But the typical situation still remains something of a half-way house. If the organisation is involved in delivering formal qualifications, the workshops that the coaches attend are likely to focus on the principles of assessment rather than learning. And when the focus of the event *is* on learning the scope tends to be limited. They may include some ideas on how to demonstrate tasks or how to listen to people but they are less likely to encourage the coach to think in terms of incidental learning and learning episodes. The support they are given is usually designed to help them to reach a minimum standard – no more than that. It is as if an expedition has reached base camp with no very clear intention of going on to the summit.

Towards a manifesto for powerful learners

Clearly we think that many organisations can and should go at least one step further. We are not advocating that the provision of direct workplace support should become a specialist role reserved for designated trainers. Far from it; moving towards a collective approach to learning demands that helping each other to learn must be seen as a shared responsibility. But we do think that there is a place for greater 'professionalism'.

Let's just for a moment think back to the checklist of criteria for auditing the learning climate in an organisation, introduced in Chapter 4:

- People are valued.

- Learning has priority.

■ There is an atmosphere of teamwork and support.

■ People are prepared to admit and learn from mistakes.

■ People are encouraged to try out new approaches.

■ Questions are welcomed and encouraged.

■ Everyone learns all the time.

How can these criteria help? In two ways. Firstly, the people who have learning support written into their job description – and we hope there will be many more of them – can use both these criteria and the other ideas in this section to reflect on their practice and to critically evaluate their contribution to the workplace as a learning environment.

And there is a second point. This chapter has painted a big picture. It began by looking back at the last century – at the abuse of knowledge revealed in the butchery of the Somme and the barbarism of fascism. But we end by looking forward. It was Tom Peters and Robert Waterman who coined the idea of 'small wins' to describe progress in organisations. We hope that everyone reading this book can look for small wins in any or all of these areas – raising the profile of learning in this way will help organisations to gain the full benefit of the three Es: economy, empowerment and enjoyment.

A career in learning?

One final thought.

This book has been written for managers and professionals, so the focus has inevitably been on how you can improve your performance in the work role. But each of us takes part in many other activities which have real importance in our lives. So, at various points, your family, membership of a community group, a club or society or involvement in an 'amateur' activity such as sport or drama may be at least as important to you as paid employment.

In his later work Donald Super recognised that these differing life roles vary in importance at different points in an individual's career. We suspect that he felt that in an ideal world other roles would gradually take over from paid employment as we approach retirement. Whether this is the case or not, throughout your life you will learn valuable lessons from *every* aspect of your life. The closing point we should like to make is this. A dynamic approach to learning could turn out to be one of the most important threads which runs through these different activities, making connections between each and every one of them.

Enjoy making the connections!

References

Abbott, J. (1977) 'To be intelligent', in *Education 2000*.

Argyris, C. (1985) *Strategy, Change and Defensive Routines,* Pitman.

Armbruster, B.B., 'Metacognition in creativity', in. Glover, J.A, R.R. Ronning and C.R. Reynolds (Eds), *Handbook of Creativity*, Plenum Press.

Bannister, D. and Fransella, F. (1971) *Inquiring Man*, Penguin.

Bates, A.W. (Tony) (1995) *Technology*, Open Learning and Distance Education, Routledge.

Benner, P. (1984) *From Novice to Expert: Excellence and Power in Clinical Nursing Practice*, Addison Wesley.

Benner, P. and Tanner, C. (1987) 'Clinical judgement: How expert nurses use intuition', *American Journal of Nursing*, 1.

Bentley, T. (1994) *Facilitation: Providing Opportunities for Learning*, McGraw Hill.

Biggs, J. (1988) 'Approaches to learning and essay writing', in Schmeck, R.R. (Ed), *Learning Strategies and Learning Styles*, Plenum Press.

Blagg, N. and Lewis, R. (1993) *Thinking and Learning at Work*, DfEE.

Boud, R., Keogh, R. and Walker, D. (1985) *Reflection: Turning Experience into Learning*, Kogan Page.

Britain Yearly Meeting (1995) *Quaker Faith and Practice*, The Religious Society of Friends.

Buzan, A. (1995) *Use Your Head*, BBC.

Campaign for Learning (1998) *Working to Create an Appetite for Learning*, Campaign for Learning.

Chambers, E. (1994) 'Assessing learner workload', in Lockwood, F., *Materials Production in Open and Distance Learning*, Paul Chapman Publishing.

Cherry, N. (1976) 'Persistent job changing – is it a problem?', *Journal of Occupational Psychology*, 49.

Coffey, J. (1977) 'Open learning opportunities for mature adults' in Davies, T.C. (Ed), *Open Learning for Mature Adults*, Council for Educational Technology.

Coopersmith, S. (1967) *The Antecedents of Self Esteem*, San Francisco, W. H. Freeman.

Crafts Council (Edited by J. Egglston) (1988) *Learning through Making: A National Enquiry into the Value of Creative, Practical Education*, Crafts Council.

Crozier, W.R. (1992) *Individual Learners: Personality Differences in Education*, London, Routledge.

Dacey, J.S. (1976) *New Ways to Learn*, Greystoke.

De Bono, E. (1973) *The Use of Lateral Thinking*, Jonathan Cape.

Dean, R.S. (1977) 'Effects of self-concept on learning with gifted children', *Journal of Educational Research*, 70.

Deming, W.E. (1986) *Out of the Crisis*, Cambridge University Press.

Department of Health (1991) *Research for Health: A Research and Development Strategy for the NHS*, HMSO.

Dewey, J. (1916) *Democracy and Education: An Introduction to the Philosophy of Education*, Macmillan.

Dewey, J. (1933) *How We Think*, D. C. Heath.

Entwhistle, N. (1988) 'Motivational factors in students' approach to study', in Schmeck, R.R. (Ed), *Learning Strategies and Learning Styles*, Plenum Press.

Finke, R.A., (1995) 'Creative realism', in Smith, S.M., T.B. Ward and R.A. Finke (Eds), *The Creative Cognition Approach*, Massachusetts Institute of Technology.

Fitzgerald, M. (1994) 'Theories of reflection for learning', in Palmer, A., S. Burns and C. Bulman, *Reflective Practice in Nursing*, Blackwell.

Flanagan, J. (1954) 'The critical incident technique', *Psychological Bulletin*, 51.

Fowler, J. and Chevannes, M. (1998) 'Evaluating the efficacy of reflective practice within the context of clinical supervision', *Journal of Advanced Nursing*, 27.

Freeman, R. and Meed, J. (1999) *How to Study Effectively*, National Extension College.

Freire, P. (1972) *Pedagogy of the Oppressed*, Continuum.

Freire, P. (1974) *Education: The Practice of Freedom*, Writers and Readers Publishing Cooperative.

Freud, S. (1901) *The Psychopathology of Everyday Life*, Penguin.

Fritz, R. (1994) *The Path of Least Resistance*, Butterworth-Heinemann.

Gagné, R.M. (1985) *The Conditions of Learning and the Theory of Instruction* (4th edition), Holt, Rinehart, Winston.

Gagné, R.M. (1989) 'Some reflections on individual differences', in Ackerman, P., R. Sternberg and R. Glaser. (Eds), *Learning and Individual Differences*, Freeman and Co.

Garratt, B. (1990) *Creating a Learning Organisation*, Director Books.

Gibbs, G. (1981) *Teaching Students to Learn: A Student Centered Approach*, Oxford University Press.

Gibbs, G. (1988) *Learning by Doing: A Guide to Teaching and Learning Methods*, Further Education Unit, Oxford Polytechnic.

Gibbs, G., Morgan, A., and Taylor, E. (1988) 'The world of the learner', in Schmeck, R.R. (Ed), *Learning Strategies and Learning Styles*, Plenum Press.

Greene, M. and Gibbons, A. (1991) 'Learning logs for self development', *Training and Development*, February.

Guildford, J.P. (1977) 'Way beyond the IQ', The Creative Education Foundation.

Habermas, J. (1972) *Knowledge and Human Interests*, Heinemann, London.

Hampshire, S. (1965) *Thought and Action*, Chatto and Windus.

Handy, C. (1993) *Understanding Organisations*, Penguin Business.

Harré, R. and Secord, P.F. (1972) *The Explanation of Social Behaviour*, Basil Blackwell.

Heath, R. (1964) *The Reasonable Adventurer*, University of Pittsburgh Press.

Heron, J. (1981) 'Self and peer assessment', in Boydler, T. and M. Pedler, *Management Self Development Concepts and Practice*, Gower.

Herzberg, F. (1968) 'One more time: how do you motivate employees?', *Harvard Business Review*, Jan–Feb.

Hill, C. (1972) *The World Turned Upside Down*, Penguin.

Hoggart, R. (1953) *The Uses of Literacy*, Penguin.

Holt, J. (1965) *How Children Fail*, Pitman.

Holt, J. (1965) *How Children Learn*, Pitman.

Honey, P. and Mumford, A. (1976) *The Manual of Learning Styles*, Peter Honey Publications.

Hopson, B. and Scally, M. (1979) *The Adult as a Developing Person: Implications for Helpers*, CRAC.

Horkheimer, M. and Adorno, T.W. (1973) The *Dialectic of Enlightenment*, Allen Lane.

Hudson, L. (1966) *Contrary Imaginations*, Penguin.

Hudson, L. (1968) *Frames of Mind*, Penguin.

Illich, I. (1971) *Deschooling Society*, Penguin.

Jacques, E., Gibson, R.O. and Isaac, D.J. (Eds) (1978) *Levels of Abstraction in Logic and Human Action*, Heinemann.

Jenkins, J. (1981) *Materials for Learning – How to Teach Adults at a Distance*, Routledge and Kegan Paul.

Johns, C.C. (1992) 'The Burford Nursing Development Unit holistic model of nursing practice', *Journal of Advanced Nursing*, 16.

Jung, C.G. (1965) *Analytical Psychology: Its Theory and Practice*, Ark.

Kakabadse, A., Ludlow, R. and Vinnicombe, S. (1988) *Working in Organisations*, Penguin.

Kanter, R.M. (1985) *The Change Masters*, Counterpoint.

Kanter, R.M. (1989) *When Giants Learn to Dance*, Simon and Schuster.

Kelly, G.A. (1955) *The Psychology of Personal Constructs*, Norton.

Kelly, G.A. (1970) 'Behaviour is an experiment', in Banister, D. (Ed), *Perspectives in Personal Construct Theory*, Academic Press.

Kirby, J.R. (1998) 'Style, strategy and skill in reading', in Schmeck, R.R. (Ed), *Learning Strategies and Learning Styles*, Plenum Press.

Knasel, E.G. (1997) *Key Skills in Modern Apprenticeships: Royal United Hospital*, Department for Education and Employment.

Knasel, E.G. and Meed, J. (1994) *Becoming Competent: Effective Learning for Occupational Competence*, Department for Education and Employment.

Kneller, G.F. (1965) *The Art and Science of Creativity*, Holt, Reinehart and Winston.

Kock, W.E. (1978) *The Creative Engineer: The Art of Inventing*, Plenum Press.

Kolb, D.A. (1984) *Experiential Learning: Experience as a Source of Learning and Development*, Prentice Hall.

Kuhn, T.S. (1962) *The Structure of Scientific Revolutions*, University of Chicago.

L'Aiguille, Y. (1994) 'Pushing back the boundaries of personal experience', in Palmer, A., S. Burns and C. Bulman, *Reflective Practice in Nursing*, Blackwell.

Law, B. (1996) 'A career-learning theory', in Watts, A.G., B. Law, J. Killeen, J.M. Kidd and R. Hawthorn, *Rethinking Careers Education and Guidance*, Routledge.

Law, B. and Watts, A.G. (1977) *Schools, Careers and Community*, Church Information Office.

Lawrence, D. (1988) *Enhancing Self Esteem in the Classroom*, Paul Chapman Publishing.

Learning Declaration Group (1998) *A Declaration on Learning*, Peter Honey.

Levinson, D. J., Darrow, C.M., Klein, B.B., Levinson, M.H. and McKee, B. (1978) *The Seasons of a Man's Life*, Alfred Knopf.

Lewin, K. (1951) *Field Theory in Social Science*, Harper & Row.

Lewis, C. (1936) *Sagittarius Rising*, Warner Books.

Lewis, R. and Paine, N. (1985) *How to Communicate with the Learner*, Council for Education Technology.

Lewis, R. and Spencer, D. (1985) *What is Open Learning*, Council for Educational Technology.

McCarthy, P. and Schmeck, R.R. (1988) 'Students' self concepts and the quality of learning in public schools and universities', in Schmeck, R.R. (Ed), *Learning Strategies and Learning Styles*, Plenum Press.

McKeachie, W.J. (1988) 'The need for study skills training', in Weinstein, C.E., E.T. Goetz and P.A. Alexander (Eds), *Learning and Study Strategies*, Academic Press.

McKinnon, D.W. (1962), 'The nature and nurture of creative talent', *American Psychologist*, 17.

Marsick, V. (1987) *Learning in the Workplace*, Croom Helm.

Marton, F., and Saljo, R. (1984) 'Approaches to learning', in Marton, F., D. Hounsell and N. Entwhistle (Eds), *The Experience of Learning*, Scottish Academic Press.

Marx, K. (1988) *Economic and Philosophic Manuscripts of 1844*, Prometheus Books.

Mednick, S. (1962), 'The associative basis of the creative process', *Psychology Review*, 69.

National Advisory Committee on Creative and Cultural Education (1999) *All Our Futures: Creativity, Culture and Education*, DfEE.

NHS Executive (1993) *A Vision for the Future*, Department of Health.

Office for National Statistics (1998) *Living in Britain: Results from the 1996 General Household Survey*, Stationery Office.

Osborn, A.F. (1963) *Applied Imagination*, Charles Scribner's Sons.

Pask, G. (1988) 'Learning strategies, teaching strategies and conceptual or learning styles', in Schmeck, R.R. (Ed), *Learning Strategies and Learning Styles*, Plenum Press.

Peters, T. (1999) 'The brand called You', *Fast Company*, 10.

Peters, T. and Austin, N. (1985) *A Passion for Excellence*, Random House.

Peters, T. and Waterman, R. (1982) *In Search of Excellence*, HarperCollins.

Piaget, J. (1972) *Psychology and Epistemology: Towards a Theory of Knowledge*, Penguin.

Piaget, J. and Inhelder, B. (1969) *The Psychology of the Child*, Routledge and Kegan Paul.

Powell, J. P. (1985) 'Autobiographical learning', in Boud, R., R. Keogh and D. Walker, *Reflection: Turning Experience into Learning*, Kogan Page.

Race, P. (1986) *How to Win as an Open Learner*, Council for Educational Technology.

Race, P. and Bourner, T. (1995) *How to Win as a Part-time Student*, Kogan Page.

Ramsden, P. (1988) 'Context and strategy: situational influences on learning', in Schmeck, R.R. (Ed), *Learning Strategies and Learning Styles*, Plenum Press.

Reissman, F. (1972) 'The strategy of style', in Sperry, L., *Learning Performance and Individual Differences*, Scott Foresman.

Rogers, A. (1996) *Teaching Adults* (2nd edition), Open University Press.

Rogers, C.R. (1961) *On Becoming a Person*, Constable.

Rogers, C.R. (1983) *Freedom to Learn for the 80's*, Merrill.

Rogers, J. (1989) *Adults Learning* (3rd edition), Open University Press.

Rossetti, A.L.I., Meed, J. and Knasel, E.G. (1996) *Learning by Design*, DfEE.

Rowntree, D. (1994) *Preparing Materials for Open, Distance and Flexible Learning*, Open University Press.

Ruddock, J. (1978) *Learning through Small Group Discussion*, Society for Research into Higher Education, University of Surrey.

Saljo, R. (1982) *Learning and Understanding: A Study of Differences in Constructing Meaning from a Text*, Acta Universitatis Gothoburgensis.

Sargent, N. (1997) *The Learning Divide*, NIACE.

Saylor, C.R. (1990) 'Reflection and professional education: art, science and competency', *Nurse Educator*, 15.

Schmeck, R.R. and Meier, S.T. (1984) 'Self-reference as a learning strategy and a learning style', *Human Learning*, 3.

Schön, D.A. (1983) *The Reflective Practitioner: How Professionals Think in Action*, Basic Books.

Schonberger, R.J. (1982) *Japanese Manufacturing Techniques*, Free Press.

Schonberger, R.J. (1990) *Building a Chain of Customers*, Hutchinson.

Scottish Consultative Council on the Curriculum (1996), *Teaching for Effective Learning*, SCCC.

Sheehy, G. (1976) *Passages: Predictable Crises of Adult Life*, E. P. Dutton.

Shotter, J. (1970) 'Men, the man makers', in *Perspectives in Personal Construct Theory*, Academic Press.

Sims, R.S. (1996) 'The search for purpose in correspondence education', in *The Brandenbury Memories Essays in Correspondence Instruction*, University of Wisconsin.

Singh, S. (1997) *Fermat's Last Theorem*, Fourth Estate.

Skinner, B.F. (1948) *Walden Two*, Macmillan Publishing.

Skinner, B.F. (1953) *Science and Human Behavior*, Free Press.

Skinner, B.F. (1954) 'The science of learning and the art of teaching', *Harvard Educational Review*.

Skinner, B.F. (1971) *Beyond Freedom and Dignity*, Penguin.

Smith, R.M. (1983) *Learning How to Learn – Applied Theory for Adults*, Open University Press.

Stern, M.I. *Stimulating Creativity*, Academic Press Inc.

Super, D.E. (1957) *The Psychology of Careers*, Harper and Row.

Super, D.E. (1980) 'A life span, life space approach to career development', in *Journal of Vocational Behaviour*, 16.

Super, D.E. and Bohn, M.J. (1971) *Occupational Psychology*, Tavistock.

Super, D.E. and Knasel, E.G. (1981) 'Career development in adulthood: some theoretical problems and a possible solution', *British Journal of Guidance and Counselling*, 9.

Super, D.E. and Thompson, A.S. (1979) 'A six-scale, two factor measure of vocational maturity', *Vocational Guidance Quarterly*.

Svensson, L. (1976) *Study Skill and Learning*, Acta Universitatis Gothoburgensis.

Sylva, K. and Moss, P. (1992) *Learning Before School*, National Commission on Education.

Tansey, G. and Worsley, P. (1995) *The Food System: A Guide*, Earthscan.

Tawney, R.H. (1931) *Equality*, Unwin.

Torrence, E. and Ellis Paul, P. (1971) *Creative Teaching and Learning*, Harper and Row.

Vygotski, L.S. (1978) *Mind in Society: The Development of Higher Psychological Processes*, Harvard University Press.

Weber, M. (1947) *The Theory of Social and Economic Organisation*, Free Press.

Weinstein, C.E. and Underwood, V.L. (1985) 'Learning strategies: the how of learning', in Segal, J.W., S.F. Chipman and R. Glaser, *Thinking and Learning skills: Volume 1 Relating Instruction to Research*, Lawrence Erlbaum Associates.

Weinstein, C.E., Zimmerman, S.A. and Palmer, R.P. (1988) 'The design and development of the LASSI', in Schmeck, R.R. (Ed), *Learning Strategies and Learning Styles*, Plenum Press.

Weinstein, C.E., Goetz, E.T. and Alexander, P.A. (Eds) (1988) *Learning and Study Strategies*, Academic Press.

Wilson, A. (1995) *Individual Commitment to Learning – Making it Happen*, Employment Department.

Wilson-Thomas, L. (1995) 'Applying critical social theory in nursing education to bridge the gap between theory, research and practice', *Journal of Advanced Nursing*, 21.

Winne, P.H., Woodlands, M.J. and Wong, B.Y.L. (1982) 'Comparability of self concept among learning disabled, normal and gifted students', *Journal of Learning Disabilities*, 15.

Woodlett, A. and Parlett, M. (1983) 'Student drop-out', *Teaching at a Distance*, 24.

Index